WORTH REPEATING
WORTH REPEATING
WORTH REPEATING
WORTH REPEATING
WORTH REPEATING
WORTH REPEATING
WORTH REPEATING
WORTH REPEATING

WORTH REPEATING

San Antonio Stories

Edited by
Paul Flahive
Tori Pool
and Burgin Streetman

MAVERICK BOOKS / TRINITY UNIVERSITY PRESS
San Antonio

Published by Maverick Books, an imprint of Trinity University Press
San Antonio, Texas 78212

Copyright © 2023 Texas Public Radio

Cover design by DeuxSouth
Book design by BookMatters, Berkeley

A slightly different version of Sheila Black's "Passing My Disability" appeared in "Modern Love," *New York Times*, Sept. 11, 2016, and in *About Us: Essays from the Disability Series of the New York Times* (Liveright, 2019); Norma Cantú's "Oreo" appeared as "Vida de perro / A Dog's Life" in *Chicana/Latina Studies* 14, no. 2 (Spring 2015); a slightly different version of Kelly Grey Carlisle's "My Mother Was Thinking of Me" appeared as "What He Took" in the *Rumpus*, June 20, 2012; Lorenzo Gomez III's "The Beatdown That Wasn't" was taken from several stories in his book *Tafolla Toro: Three Years of Fear* (Geekdom Media, 2019).

978-1-59534-994-1 paper
978-1-59534-995-8 ebook

Printed in Canada

Trinity University Press strives to produce its books using methods and materials in an environmentally sensitive manner. We favor working with manufacturers that practice sustainable management of all natural resources, produce paper using recycled stock, and manage forests with the best possible practices for people, biodiversity, and sustainability. The press is a member of the Green Press Initiative, a nonprofit program dedicated to supporting publishers in their efforts to reduce their impacts on endangered forests, climate change, and forest-dependent communities.

The paper used in this publication meets the minimum requirements of the American National Standard for Information Sciences—Permanence of Paper for Printed Library Materials, ansi 39.48–1992.

CIP data on file at the Library of Congress

27   26   25   24   23 | 5   4   3   2   1

Contents

Introduction

PAUL FLAHIVE

I was asked to write about how *Worth Repeating* was created at Texas Public Radio—a story about a storytelling program that tells people's stories. Unfortunately, that story isn't one of long deliberative contemplation and analysis, surveys sent to community groups, and thoughtful discussion on what San Antonio needs. It came fully formed.

In short, it is a rip-off. A rip-off of a rip-off, truth be told.

The story of *Worth Repeating* coming to Texas is the same as my own story of coming to the state. And it starts in Alaska.

"What the fuck am I doing here?"

That was on my mind one night in downtown Anchorage. It was cold...which in Alaska is sort of like saying it was daytime, or nighttime, or we existed.

But it *was* cold. It was one of those cold months in Alaska—one of ten of them—and I was grudgingly meeting a former-girlfriend-now-just-friend for a drink and a show. It was a Monday, which was one of my days off from my job at a homeless shelter for teens, and frankly I didn't want to be there. I didn't want to hang out with a woman I had just broken things off with after a few months and get a drink and go to a weird little theater on the edge of downtown for a show about—well, something. See? I had forgotten what I was even going to.

"What the fuck am I doing here?" was on my mind. But not just about being downtown. What was I doing in Alaska?

Don't get me wrong. I love Alaska, and the people are friendly. I made some of my best friends during my time there, and summers (all two months of them) are phenomenal, and the camping is great. But to quote Raymond Carver, "What's in Alaska?" I mean, what's in the state—for me—as a life? It didn't seem like much.

I didn't seem to fit. I hated skiing. I don't work in the oil industry or for the World Wildlife Fund. I was twenty-six, and every other moment was an existential crisis about my future. I was writing less-than-engaging arts features for the local paper a couple times a month and working at a homeless shelter for kids.

What brought me to the state was so silly as to be barely worth mentioning. In the previous few years I had gone through three girlfriends, as many jobs, and a graduate program, all without much to show for the time.

The fact that I was working with kids in deplorable situations made the whole quarter-life crisis thing especially precious and asinine. Regardless, I was annoyed, as I often am, and not wanting to be there. I was standing outside waiting for my ex to show up and steam was coming out of my nose because—again—it was Alaska.

The theater was Cyrano's Playhouse, on Fourth Street across from a strange, canary-yellow building boasting a covered market that was usually empty, and next door to a rather grimy bar that my friends and I often found ourselves in toward the end of the night.

My ex had bought the tickets, and the conversation was pretty stilted as we sipped the free drink that came with the ticket. If my memory serves, this was the first time we'd hung out since I said we should hang it up. I asked her what the show was about; she told me it was live storytelling and immediately started trying to keep me from walking out.

What self-indulgence. My cringe did not subside even after we were seated and the program started.

Cyrano's was a tiny little black box theater space. I remember it being comfortable with around fifty people in there, and had it reached capacity I would have had to inhale sharply and hold my breath. "Intimate" is likely the word on the marketing materials.

Before long, hosts James Keck and Tara Loyd were telling us what the show was and why it existed. They said they had ripped it off from a show in Baltimore called

Stoop Stories. The stoop in that city is where the stories are told. In Alaska it's inside, so they called the show *Arctic Entries*.

The two, who met in graduate school at Johns Hopkins, had loved the show and thought they could probably pull it off in their spare time. Keck was a so-called disease detective for the CDC. And Tara was working at a few places but also volunteering.

The truth is, Tara was actually one of my volunteers on the shelter's street outreach team and had told me about the show several times. When she walked onstage, I was embarrassed that I had completely forgotten.

This was one of the first shows they did since arriving the previous spring.

My cringe lessened. Tara is one of those people who genuinely likes other people and wants to help them. All the profits went to a local nonprofit. James has a quirky sense of humor, and the two generated genuine warmth.

The show started, and a guy with an acoustic guitar would play between stories.

It was stripped down. A black floor surrounded by seats. A couple of spotlights. No microphone because the room was so small, and just a person standing there telling a story. A sad or funny or meandering should-have-been-better-edited story.

Before long I was laughing. I was not on the edge of my seat but was really quite engaged.

I was thinking to myself, *What the fuck is this doing here?*

After they made it through their scheduled slate of storytellers, they invited people from the audience to come up. And it was at this point that I heard genuinely one of the most filthy stories of my life. I won't repeat it here, but it involved the Mississippi Delta, an old woman, and "the vines."

I started to feel something too. I looked around at the intent faces. People were interested and engaged. People were laughing, sometimes over very cheesy things. It was warm. It was inviting. It was a community. After years in the small wintry city, I felt a comfort I'd rarely sensed before.

When the show ended, I walked up to Tara and asked why it wasn't being recorded.

I had worked for several years in public radio and had been a journalist, engineer, station manager, what have you. I volunteered to record the whole thing. I bought all the equipment myself, and the next show was recorded (mostly—there were some technical difficulties involving a very energetic storyteller and a body mic). I kept doing it.

When James and Tara moved to Africa to run a clinic the following year, I volunteered to help keep things going. The show grew: the audience doubled in size, and we had to get a new venue. When I got an offer to work at Texas Public Radio later that year, it was one of the few things that made me question the move to San Antonio.

A few years later, when a young underwriting rep at the station told me she had been tasked with finding an event geared toward younger listeners, I told her about my very ripped-off plan for a live storytelling show.

"*The Sound of San Antonio* through the stories of your friends and neighbors" was the line I used in the pitch meeting with the CEO, Joyce Slocum, and a few others.

I told an annotated version of the story above, adding that it wasn't until I found the show that Anchorage began to feel like my home. I thought the show was something we could give to the community while enlisting the support of hundreds of people who had lived here for years.

As I sit writing this, seven years after the show launched and a dozen years after I first stumbled into Cyrano's, it still surprises me how much of that feeling I remember. It surprises me how much of that same feeling our show has managed to generate, and how generous the audiences continue to be.

Hundreds of San Antonio stories have been told through *Worth Repeating*. Vulnerable stories of loss and pain and grief. Funny stories of mistakes.

People still listen in, excited to hear more. They're generous with laughter and applause. And that comfort and that community continue to grow.

And we're always looking for more—to continue to weave the sound of the city.

The stories that fill these pages are some of our favorites. We hope you like them.

Will You Go with Me?

HEATHER ARMSTRONG

I was an ugly kid.

Okay, maybe not ugly, but the kind where your relatives just can't bring themselves to say you're pretty, so they call you sweet.

Don't worry. It got better.

Third grade wasn't kind to me, as that's when my nose grew before the rest of my face. Not helping matters, mullets were in style. Naturally, I got one.

"Why would you do something like that?" my mom cried when I got back from the beauty shop. "Your hair looks awful. Awwfulll."

The worst part about my awkward stage is that I was tall. By fifth grade, I was about five-eight. I got tall so fast that body parts didn't grow together at the same time. In our photo albums, my arms look like those of an ape, hanging down to my knees alongside legs that hadn't sprouted yet. I also had zero chest, so I truly looked like a boy—especially with that mullet. I look back at pictures and can't fathom how my parents still loved me.

All I wanted was a boyfriend. There weren't a lot of prospects, but I found him. Of all the boys in the school, there was only one taller than me: Ernie. Ernie was dumber than a sack of hammers, had a constant look of surprise on his open-mouthed face, and was constantly failing classes (how do you fail fifth-grade art class?), but he was taller than me, and that was all that mattered.

Just days before fifth grade came to a close, I returned from recess to find my friend Tiffany, who put a note in my hand. I opened it up, and behold: the Most Amazing Note in the Entire Universe. Scrawled in a scritch-scratch was the question: "wil you go with me!" Then three boxes: one for yes, one for no, one for "maybye." "Love, Ernie." Love, Ernie!

A rush of love, excitement, and pure adrenaline zoomed through me so fiercely, I was afraid Mrs. Hankhamer was going to see my heart leaping out of my chest. I couldn't contain myself. I whipped out my pencil, checked the box for yes, and got it back to Tiffany in seconds. She had such a huge smile on her face. I could tell she was happy for me and Ernie.

Over the next few days, Ernie never acknowledged that he had received the note, but Tiffany swore up and down that she had given it to him. I sought his eyes during recess and between classes, but he never so much as glanced at me. It was as if the note had never happened. Even though I was only eleven, I had this deep, profound urge not to make myself look desperate and run after him. So, I went about my day as if every second without his attention wasn't crushing my soul and leaving me dead inside.

Summer came, and I don't remember much about the next few weeks except that my dad insisted I plow. We lived on a farm, and that year Dad was planting cotton and needed the fields plowed, so he made my sister and me work for him. I spent my days in the air-conditioned cab of the tractor daydreaming about Ernie, our relationship, how I was going to tutor him, help him get A's, how he would be so grateful to me for turning his life around, and then we would get married.

Each day that I didn't hear from him, I rationalized that he was probably having to do the same thing: work for his parents. It could be any number of things—he could be out of town at summer camp or on vacation with his family, or his phone had stopped working because of a terrible storm that knocked a tree down on his phone line. It wasn't even in my realm of possibilities that it was because he wasn't my boyfriend. I mean, I checked the box that said yes.

Then one day my mother told me Tiffany had called and invited me to her swim party that coming Saturday. Oh my God, I'm going to see Ernie! I didn't even need Tiffany to respond because I knew he would be there, and I would finally be able to be his girlfriend, like, in front of people!

The days slogged along until Saturday rolled around. Two o'clock finally arrived, and I decided to show up a few minutes late, so as to make a grand entrance. As I walked to the pool, I imagined the knowing look on Ernie's face, our eventual embrace, and the silly little games we would play with each other. I pictured all the girls' faces when they saw Ernie and me arm-in-arm, teasing each other, jealous that I had the tallest guy in the school.

And then I arrived.

There was Ernie, sitting in a chair with Tiffany in his lap. In his lap! My heart sank. I was so stunned that I had to stop and take a deep breath for a second. I gathered myself and approached, trying to smile.

"Hey, y'all," I muttered.

Nothing from Ernie except his usual surprised look with his mouth wide open. But Tiffany was smiling, and it wasn't a *hey, friend* smile. It was a little shit-eating grin.

"So, hey, Ernie." I smiled.

The entire group of kids started laughing. Even Ernie. *Especially* Tiffany. She pointed at me, screaming with delight. Not having a clue what was so funny, I started laughing too.

"No, dummy, we're laughing *at you*. You think Ernie is your boyfriend!" she said, in between gulps of air and laughing.

"What?" I said, and felt a sting in my throat.

"You think Ernie really wanted to go with you. But he was just kidding! And you fell for it!" Tiffany blurted. The whole group started to laugh again.

Somehow, as if I knew it all along, I started laughing and said, "Why would you think that? I totally knew! Oh my God, Tiffany! Like, seriously!"

To this day, I have no idea how I pulled that out of my shattered self.

The next few moments are hazy. I recall jumping off the high dive, joking with other kids in the water, laughing— all the while feeling like I was having a heart attack and wanting to die. I laughed off the repeated questions—"Did you really think Ernie was your boyfriend?"—until they finally stopped. I wasn't going to cry.

I remember seeing Tiffany and Ernie flirting, hanging out arm-in-arm, teasing each other, and playing out the scenes that I had created in my mind. Except Ernie was doing it with Tiffany and not me.

Finally, I couldn't fake it any longer, so I grabbed my towel, told the kids goodbye, and walked home, crying every step of the way. Not only did I not have a boyfriend, but I was a joke to all those kids. I realized the only reason Tiffany invited me was so they could make fun of me.

I was a fool. A brokenhearted, embarrassed fool.

Here's where most people will tell you how this moment changed them, or how it was a turning point in their life, or how this emotional reckoning altered their understanding of love. No—I figure you want to know what happened to those assholes. Ernie ended up in prison, and Tiffany...well, I'll be nice. She's sweet, I'll tell you that.

Millionaire Slumdog

TANVEER ARORA

My name is Tanveer Arora. You probably could have guessed by my name that I'm not originally from San Antonio. That's right, I'm actually from Laredo, Texas. How disappointed would you be if I said I was kidding, that I'm actually from India? A little bit, right?

I am from India. I grew up there, spent twenty-two years of my life there, then decided to move to America. I still remember my first day when I landed at the airport in Houston. The TSA person looks at my passport and reads India, and he goes, "I watched *Slumdog Millionaire* recently. And it's a pretty hard life." And I was like, yes. It *is* a pretty hard life.

Honestly, I faced a lot of hardships growing up in India. I'll tell you a few. For starters, I grew up in Mumbai. If you don't know what Mumbai is or where it is, just imagine New York City but with Indian people. And my parents, they weren't that wealthy. We only had a two-story house in the heart of Mumbai. And we only had five cars. And each car came with a dedicated driver. I never got to drive. It was really hard, you guys. Really hard. And we only had five maids, you know? I remember one was for cleaning, one was for cooking, one was for laundry, one was for dishes, and one was just a backup.

I remember when I was a teenager watching this Bollywood movie. There's this actor, and he had this round bed—never seen that in my life, a round bed. And I told my dad, that's what I want. And guess what? They don't sell round beds in stores. Like I said, it was pretty hard for us. My dad had to custom make a round bed for me. And once that bed was made, we realized they didn't sell round bedsheets in stores, so he had to custom make those as well.

It was a sweet, sweet life that I gave up. I don't know why. It was actually really good. I guess I got greedy. I thought, *How do I take this experience to the next level?* I googled "Which is the best city in the entire world," and New York City popped up. I didn't know much about the entire world. I was just in my bubble. So, I did all my research on New York City, and by research I mean I watched all ten seasons of *Friends*. Then I googled "how to enter the United States of America." A lot of articles showed up on how to cross the border from Mexico. That wasn't what I was looking for. No, I found out the best way to come to America was to enroll at a university for, say, a graduate program. That's what I did. I applied to a bunch of colleges. I got an acceptance letter from a university in New York, and it was pretty expensive. My parents said they were not going to pay for it. They would not do it.

They wanted me to live with them for life, so my American Dream was kind of shattered.

But I still had enough motivation to move out of India. One of the biggest motivations to move out was this group of people that always meddle in my life. All my Hispanic friends, you guys would know: you call them relatives. I just had to move. I got lucky and got an acceptance letter from Texas A&M University in College Station, and my future changed. They offered me a scholarship and also a stipend every week. I thought, *This is a no-brainer*. My parents warned, "If you want to do this, you're on your own." I said, fine, let's do this. College Station. How different can that be from New York City? I mean, it's America, so it has to be the same, right? Almost the same.

I took a flight to Houston and then a shuttle to College Station. I got out of the shuttle. I took a stroll in College Station, and I legit thought, *I'm in a time-travel movie. I've gone back in time. Way, way back in time.* I was looking for those tall buildings. I was looking for those flashy lights. Where are my Times Square flashy lights? Forget flashy lights, there weren't even streets like that in College Station. But my apartment was actually pretty close to what I had in Mumbai. We didn't have a round bed; instead, we had an eighty-year-old carpet that I slept on. And we didn't have a TV in every room like my house in Mumbai. But the walls were so thin I could hear my neighbor's TV and my roommate's TV, so it was free entertainment. It was pretty sweet.

I've always wondered, was it a wise decision to start all over again? Because in that apartment, I was the one to clean. I was the one to cook. I was the one to do laundry. I was the one to do dishes, all by myself. And I got a second-hand car that I had to drive myself. If you think about it, my story is also like *Slumdog Millionaire*...just in reverse.

Turkey Royalty

JENNIE BADGER

It may shock you to learn that I am royalty. I mean, I'm no Meghan Markle. You'll never see me splashed across the cover of some highfalutin New York fashion magazine or profiled in a hoity-toity society publication. You've never even asked me to show you my shoes at a Fiesta parade. But like *that* fake royalty, I too have a crown and a title no one can take away from me. That's right: I am the first-ever, the original—the OG as the young kids call it—Little. Miss. Cuero. You may bow.

I come from Cuero, Texas, a small town about ninety miles southeast of San Antonio. I was five years old when I nabbed the title of child queen for my hometown, whose motto is "Cuero, Texas—Where America Talks Turkey," and whose billboards proudly proclaim it "Turkey Capital of the World." If you haven't guessed by now, Cuero used to be known for its turkey farms, and it was also known for its...turkey farms. As a result, everything there either is named for or revolves around that heritage.

That is why the high school mascot is a Gobbler. It's really a *Fighting* Gobbler, because only Cuero would make the dumbest animal in the entire world its mascot, then draw it to look like a big old, Hulked-up, steroid-injected piece of poultry that every athletic team should fear. That mind game must work, though, because Cuero has one of the most successful high school football programs in Texas, and you know it's because of that stupid turkey.

It is no exaggeration to say that every single thing in our high school revolved around that turkey theme. The title of our student newspaper? *Turkey Talk*. The name of our dance team? The Trotters. Prom titles? Gobbler King and Queen. You get the idea. #OnceaGobbleralwaysaGobbler.

Here's the truly amazing thing: I am not the only royal in my family. My dad enjoyed the ultimate title when in 1972, he was crowned Sultan Yekrut XIV. Now Yekrut is turkey spelled backward. He received this honor so he could reign over a four-day extravaganza known as Turkey Trot. The official title of the young woman he reigned with was Sultana Oreuc, which is Cuero spelled backward.

In fact, the Turkey Trot celebration was really an homage to the Turkish Empire, because...wait for it...Cuero had turkeys, and there is a country named Turkey. That is truly the sole connection. You cannot deny that Cueroites are a clever lot, so much so that they will build a four-day festival around a homonym.

Let me tell you a little bit about my dad. My dad was Atticus Finch before Harper Lee even knew who Atticus Finch was. He was a tall, silver-haired, small-town lawyer with black horn-rimmed glasses. He was intelligent, kind, and giving, and he had high morals. He lacked all conceit, never sought the spotlight, and didn't grandstand. That's why it's so hilarious that for four days in October 1972 he was the absolute center of attention in Cuero, and he embraced that role with great gusto.

Part of that role was to be honored with an ornate, elaborate coronation much like the opulent Fiesta coronation here in San Antonio. When he strode into the Gobbler baseball stadium as Sultan Yekrut, he looked awesome. He wore a red and gold turban and an impeccably tailored white suit under a red velvet robe with a six-inch border of gold sequins. On the back? A massive hand-beaded turkey that my aunt spent months creating.

That's not the only part of my father's coronation that mirrored that of Fiesta. Every year San Antonio's debutantes bow before the Fiesta king in their incredibly expensive gowns and robes and crowns. Cuero's young women bowed before my dad, too, but it didn't play out quite the same way. This was in part because it was 1972, and come on, it was just a completely different time. But mainly it was because in keeping with the Turkish theme, when the Cuero gals bowed before my dad, they wore harem attire. Think Barbara Eden in *I Dream of Jeannie*. For millennials, that is a midriff-baring top, sheer parachute pants, pointy-toed shoes, and a high ponytail. I think some of the women even had scarves over their faces that left only their eyes visible. Reigning over all this mayhem was my father…Atticus Finch…in a turban.

I know it sounds like a crazy 1970s acid dream, but it happened. As loony as it seems, there was something sweet and innocent about those four days of totally inappropriate cultural appropriation. Stay with me here. I was very young during Turkey Trot, but I've had a lot of time to reflect on it, and I think the reason it seems so sweet and innocent is because the world was bigger back then. No one could have imagined that one day you might push a button and visit any country in the world via a computer screen. So, they took our South Texas turkey farming heritage and wrapped it in the trappings of a culture they knew only from the resources of the time—encyclopedias and movies and novels.

You know what it was really like? A four-day dramatic production, after which everyone enjoys the cast party, turns in their costumes, and goes home, enriched by the experience and sad that it's over. That's how I feel about growing up in Cuero—so very enriched by that experience and so very sad when it was over. But you know what they say: You can take the girl out of Cuero, but you can't take Cuero out of the girl. Thank goodness! Because let's face it, without that I wouldn't be the queen I am today.

Ride-or-Die Friends

KIRAN KAUR BAINS

By my twenty-sixth birthday, I had been living and working in Gulu for a year. To celebrate, Lam and Sam were taking me to Murchison Falls, the largest park in Uganda.

I love those guys. They're my best friends. The brothers I never had. And I love birthdays—mine or anyone else's. As we drove to Murchison Falls, I felt pure joy. The kind of happiness you feel when you're with people you love and you know you have nothing but good things to look forward to. It was like going to SeaWorld with my family in the summertime, except long before *Blackfish* came out.

We had mapped and planned the whole trip. And by we, I mean Lam and Sam had mapped the whole trip: lunch, gas, and entry fees. Sam used to drive folks through the park all the time, so we didn't have to hire a guide. I offered the foolproof idea of borrowing the 1970-something sky blue Datsun pickup from the nonprofit we worked for. (Not really allowed, but still, free.)

Murchison Falls is less than an hour from Gulu, and I sat in between Sam, who was driving, and Lam, who hung out the window. I deejayed, rotating between two cassette tapes—Bob Marley's greatest hits and Bollywood jams.

As we drove into Murchison Falls, I could feel how small we were in the world—in a beautiful way. It was quiet that Wednesday morning. We didn't pass any tourists. Sam was running a tight schedule, and we hit the Nile River right on time. We watched hippos bathe while we waited for the river ferry to take us to the other side of the park. "Cuuuuuute," I remember saying. Lam and Sam, not having grown up on Disney, informed me that the hippopotamus is actually one of the deadliest mammals.

Later, when we drove off the river ferry, Sam made note of the schedule. Turned out we didn't have as much time as we thought to explore the other side of the park. Honestly, I don't remember much of what we saw there. According to Google, it was likely lions, zebras, chimpanzees, and buffalos. Maybe some cool birds. I do remember that when we got back to the Nile, the ferry boat was on the wrong side. As we waited and waited and waited, Sam, always the most chill, grew visibly anxious. His timetable was important because he couldn't navigate us out of the park at night. Not only were the dirt paths unmarked, but the animals roamed freely. At night our path would be lit by nothing more than the Datsun's headlights.

Finally, at sunset, the ferry returned. Sam sped the Datsun on and off the boat, determined to get us out of the park as quickly as possible. Then he became uncertain of his turns, taking one path, then turning around to take the other. And somehow, among these turns, night fell.

It was pitch-dark, and all of a sudden, our entire view was the midsection of an elephant. Sam, slow and steady, navigated the truck off the dirt path, into the tall grass, and around what turned out to be a mother elephant and her baby. As Sam got us back on the path, he laughed nervously and said, "Kiran, Kiran, Kiran—this is not good."

Lam had fallen silent. He had taken his shirt off as if it afforded him relief. I was taking all of my cues from Lam and Sam. They're both Acholi, natives of northern Uganda. They had come of age surviving a war and had volunteered for the World Food Programme, delivering food and water to people displaced in a remote part of the country. This, they said, would be a foolish way to die.

Sam—or was it Lam?—noticed town lights in the distance. We were determined to get closer to those lights when a pack of hyenas with piss-yellow eyes slid past the Datsun. I remember this very clearly. Lam and Sam turned to me and asked, "Kiran? Do you know the hyena?" They were asking, "Do you think hyenas are cute, too?"

We continued to drive and landed straight in a dead end, some kind of construction site. As we turned around, Sam continued to look for those town lights. Suddenly, the terrain changed. It was marshy. The Datsun's wheels began to spin—we were stuck. And then worse, the Datsun sputtered. This was not the first time the truck had broken down on us. We sat back, defeated. Both guys now had their shirts off. "Buffalo Soldier" was playing.

Sam, who I had not ever seen smoking in our one year of friendship, was holding a pack and lighting up. I had to pee. I imagined my ass getting bit by hyenas.

At some point during this time, I began calling nearby luxury hotels. Surely they had a plan in place for their guests who got lost in the park. One woman told me, "We can come get you. Do you have a credit card?" I did not have a credit card. I called my sister, who was in San Antonio, and said something like, "Hey, no time to explain..."

I'm the youngest in the family, so she had gotten used to these phone calls, sadly. Before I could call the hotel lady with my sister's credit card number, my phone rang. "Happy birthday to you," the voice sang, "Happy birthday to—"

If you are ever in crisis, the person you want by your side is my other best friend, Christina. Christina and I had graduated a year earlier from Notre Dame, where we studied peacebuilding. Christina was at a United Nations conference in Barcelona. As I explained where I was, she knew I was laughing because I was scared out of my mind. And she said, "Listen to me. I saw Betty Bigombe here in the lobby. Is this so bad that I should go ask Betty Bigombe for help?"

Betty Bigombe, known as Mama Bigombe, brokered peace talks in northern Uganda. She is a big deal. This was not how I wanted to be introduced to her in my budding peacebuilding career. Christina, ever brilliant and calm, asked how much battery I had left on my phone. She took

Lam's number and Sam's number and promised to call us back as soon as possible.

Those not-so-cute, deadly hippos? Two of them passed the Datsun that night. Lam thought it was another mother-and-baby duo, and he whispered, "Do. Not. Move." He was worried they would topple the truck.

Sometime after midnight, Betty Bigombe mobilized the national park service to search for us. The few markers we were able to offer—the dead end, the construction site, the marshy terrain, elephants, hippos, and hyenas— were enough for them to find us in less than an hour. Two Texas-sized trucks, with what felt like two dozen armed park rangers, rescued us. They put us up in a lodge for the night, fed us breakfast, and drove us back to the Datsun in the morning. They repaired the truck and, without asking any questions, escorted us out of the park.

It's been seven years since that night in Murchison Falls, and I don't like telling this story because of how it sensationalizes Africa, but one thing will always be true: my friends are ride or die.

Operation Babylift

MARION BARTH

I'm an air force wife, and in 1975 I found myself in the Philippines. I am also a mother of two, and on April 4 of that year, President Gerald Ford signed a proclamation to bring all the orphans out of Vietnam. Unfortunately, for those of us at Clark Air Base—one of the largest military installations at that time—we didn't know anything about it, so we were called to an emergency meeting at one o'clock on that Friday. We were told that that evening we would be receiving three hundred kids. There were approximately two hundred people assembled, representing sixty-three volunteer organizations at Clark, and we had nothing prepared. In this quick brainstorming session, we had to come up with ideas for how to house, transport, feed, and clothe all these kids.

And we did. It was amazing. We turned the gym into a dormitory by putting twin mattresses on the floor, two-by-two, in a checkerboard fashion. Squash courts were turned into nurseries. Other rooms were turned into depositories for donations. A call went out to all the Americans that we needed children's clothing, bottles, you name it—*now*. It came.

That evening, my job was to oversee the offloading of the orphans. All two hundred–plus volunteers assembled at the chapel, and I gave them a little briefing: one child, one volunteer.

They were told to wait until they were called, when we knew the plane was in the air. The call came in the evening, and again all two hundred volunteers assembled at the hangar. I started to give them the briefing again when someone whispered in my ear. I listened and took a deep breath. Then I said, "I'm sorry. The plane has gone down. It has crashed. We have no knowledge of how many have survived, but there are survivors. You are dismissed. You will be called again when needed. Go home and pray."

I was not allowed to go home. I was the coordinator of family services at Clark. As coordinator, I was on the deathwatch. I would visit the homes of people whose husbands didn't return. That night I went to another hangar because on these planes were wives and husbands, teenage daughters and sons, who were helping the military bring these children out of Vietnam. The rest of the families were on two other planes and had no knowledge of the crash. We had to meet the planes as they arrived and these people whose mother, father, sister, brother, whoever, might or might not be alive.

That was the beginning of Operation Babylift.

The next morning, thirty-one healthy orphans arrived. I went to the airplane and did my thing, and then they were safely on the bus. My lecture to the volunteers was something like this: "I don't care what you're getting. If it stinks, if it smells, if it spits all over you, you're to hold that child to you and hug it to your body. It could kick, it could bite—you don't do anything to it until you get on the bus. And then you can look and see what you got!"

Some of them were surprised, but they had to take the child off the down plank, across the tarmac, onto a bus. On the bus, the children were tagged so that no one was missed, because these kids were from organized orphanages in the beginning. They were headed not just to the United States but to France, England, Germany, Italy, Switzerland. These children going all over the world were wanted by other people. Genuine orphans.

The next plane came the following evening, and I did the thing again, thinking that this time I was going to get to take a child, go to the gym, and sit on a mattress with them for eight hours. It didn't happen. The chaplain said, "You did it so well the first time, let's do it again." So, I did it again. And again, and before I knew it, not only were there orphans on the plane; there were non-proper-papered people. Try to say that when you're real tired. These were refugees coming out. People who worked for the air force, or the army, or the intelligence, and they were afraid that they were going to get caught, so they were coming out. So, not only do we have these children we were taking care of, and rebooking another aircraft to go to all these places, we were having refugees showing up at Clark.

This started in April 1975. We were not finished with the evacuation of Vietnam until September. We had children coming, children going, people having babies. It was an interesting time. But the most important part of it was that we Americans, living at that time in Clark and Subic Naval Base, volunteered. We worked eight-hour shifts, went home and slept, then went back to work. You had women with children who did the same thing: go home, take care of the kids, then come back to this stint in the gym and take care of children. The hours that these people put in were astronomical. And that made me proud to be an American. Because people needed our help, and we helped them.

Passing My Disability

SHEILA BLACK

When I was six years old, Sister Agnes, the scary nun who taught religion to our first-grade class, told me I should become a nun. "A girl like you won't ever get married," she said, "so you should consider becoming a nun."

The reason she said that to me was that I had crooked legs due to a condition I was born with called X-linked hypophosphatemia, which is a name no one can say, so everyone just calls it XLH. People with XLH don't absorb phosphorus, resulting in short stature, bowed legs, soft bones, and weak teeth. I was a spontaneous case; no one in my family had ever had it before me.

I actually did not take what Sister Agnes said seriously. My mom told me there was nothing I couldn't do if I put my mind to it, and I believed her. I did worry about my legs being ugly, and I never ever wore shorts—never! And I felt weird whenever I put on a swimsuit, but despite my difficulties walking long distances—or running at all—I don't know that I thought of myself as disabled.

Until I was pregnant with my first child.

My ob-gyn immediately referred me to a genetic counselor "just in case." The counselor didn't seem too worried. "Don't sweat it," he said. "Frankly, this is so rare, you'd have to marry a guy from the rickets clinic to pass it on." His words comforted me enormously, and seven months later I gave birth to my first child—my daughter, Annabelle. And she did not have XLH.

Six years later, I stood in a neonatal intensive care unit looking down at my son, Walker. Because my husband and I had a rare RH blood incompatibility, he was born with an Apgar of only two and needed multiple blood transfusions. But what I was staring at as he lay in his incubator were his legs—something in them I recognized, a kind of curvature that felt as familiar as my own face.

"He has XLH," I said to his doctor. She said, "I wouldn't worry about that. We have enough here to worry about." But a day later she came and found me in the hall. "You were right," she said. "His phosphorus is very low. We're pretty sure he has what you have."

I mourned acutely, but briefly—mostly for the image I'd had of him as a tall, gangly teenager, the kind I had never been. Once I got over that, I never once regretted him or his XLH.

It turns out that XLH is caused by a mutation in something called the PHEX gene. When I saw the genetic counselor before Annabelle was born, the genetics of my rare condition had not yet been mapped, and in fact, the counselor was wrong. I have a 50 percent chance of passing XLH on to my children. And since the birth of Walker, I've had another daughter, Eliza, who has XLH as well.

Several years ago, a relative of mine, who is quite religious in a way I am not, called me unexpectedly. She said she wanted to apologize because she had always thought that I should never have children—God would not want you to have children, is how she put it. Yet now that I had three of them—three "beautiful children," she'd said—she wanted to let me know she had been wrong. It was kind of an awkward moment, like when someone tells you you look fabulous in a way that lets you know how truly terrible they thought you looked before.

At first I felt angry, but then I considered that for an abled person—a person who considers herself "normal"— it is probably difficult to imagine taking the risk of passing on what is considered by most to be a fairly significant disability.

The *Merck Manual of Diagnosis and Therapy* observes of XLH patients that they are "often quite robust" apart from their short stature and odd side-to-side gait, and also the pain they suffer—muscle aches, bone aches. My two younger kids and I all hover around five feet. This is not such a big deal for me and my daughter; it is more for my son, and all of us struggle if asked to stand or walk for any length of time.

Occasionally I come across the term "designer baby." It always gives me a feeling of unease. Obviously, I chose not to have designer babies—partly because, at least with my son, I never had to actually choose. My third child, Eliza, was a late, midlife accident. But I did choose to have her, despite the fifty-fifty gamble that she too would have XLH. Would I have made the same choice in a planned pregnancy or if given a choice much earlier in the process?

I am aware that some studies claim that short people score fewer points on "happiness scales," whatever that means, but my kids and I are not the average study subjects. We are just ourselves.

Sometimes people stop us and ask what is wrong with us. Most of the time I can see that people notice, but they don't say anything. Walker is more visibly disabled, which makes Eliza feel bad. She says sometimes she feels like a fraud because she has the same thing, but in her case, "You almost can't tell." Walker rides a bicycle. Eliza does yoga. Both pursue these physical activities with fierce and single-minded passion. Both do so because there are other physical activities—walking, running—that they cannot engage in without difficulty. (Ironically, the least athletic is my oldest, Annabelle, who regularly proclaims that she hates all sports.)

Pain, both physical and psychic, is a part of my kids' daily experience, and it is the part that is hardest for me to get over. Perhaps this is what my relative meant.

Most of the time, I believe my children will transcend the parts of their disability that might make them suffer. Walker might only be five feet tall, but he is in every conceivable way an engaging personality. He has friends, wild schemes for the future, a wicked, deadpan sense of humor. Eliza is all darting motion, ups and downs. She sings in the shower, does cartwheels on the lawn. She also struggles with an eating disorder and high anxiety. And Walker, normally even-keeled, occasionally gives in to fits of rage and frustration that seem to come on in particular when he grows tired of the effort of simply moving through a day, or being left out at school. In those moments, he punches walls, rides his bicycle too fast. Yet how much of this can I really blame on XLH? My oldest would not say she has a perfect life. At twenty-three, she is floundering a little—unsure of what to do with her life or how.

Sure, XLH has a cost, but so does life.

Of course, I worry about Walker and Eliza. At the same time, I experience so keenly their blazing necessity, their facticity, their utter beauty. Once I was walking along between them, and I realized all three of us possessed the exact same, awkward to most people, "disabled" way of walking. The rush of identification I felt was almost triumphant. *We don't move like other people*, I thought, *and who is to say there are not things we have learned uniquely from our way of moving or being?*

Once I asked my children how they felt about the XLH I had passed on to them. Both of them spoke of the disability as almost—though not quite—a gift.

"It has made me not fit in," Eliza said, "but it has taught me empathy."

"I'm sometimes bitter about being so short," Walker said, "and about the pain, but I am very glad to be alive."

The Hospital (and Jim Crow) Killed My Mom

BARBARA COLLINS BOWIE

My brother and I were born and raised in Jackson, Mississippi, during Jim Crow, a time of extreme racism and oppression. In 1961 my brother got involved with the civil rights movement and became a Freedom Rider. I wanted to follow him around everywhere, since he was my big brother, but he wouldn't let me. You see, he was nineteen and I was only thirteen. I knew nothing about being a Freedom Rider. I did know about the bus rides and protests because he would take me to some of his meetings when it was safe. Even though I didn't know what Freedom Riders could do to change things, one thing happened that made me understand why I needed to be involved in civil rights. I call it the "Story of My Mom."

One day I was coming home from spending time with my friends downtown. I lived on a corner, and as I was coming up my street, people were sitting on their porches. They started yelling at me, "Bobbie, Bobbie! Get home. Your mom got sick and went to the hospital!"

I was confused because we never went to the hospital. Momma always had home remedies. I went home and tried to find someone to take me, but I couldn't find anyone, so I ran there myself. It might have been two miles, but it felt like ten. When I got to the hospital, my mother and the friend who had brought her there were sitting in the emergency room. My mom looked very sick, like she was going to pass out. She had a cold, damp towel on her forehead, and she said she just didn't want to vomit again. Her friend said that she had vomited a whole wash pan full of blood. I was thinking, *I never heard of that*, so I didn't believe it. Then I asked how long they had been here. Her friend said, "We've been here since about two o'clock."

Well, at that time it was 5:30, so I went up to the desk. "My mom needs to be seen. My mom is really sick, and she's been here since two."

They were saying to me, "Well, we don't have any beds" or "We have other people we have to see." Even the doctors—you know, they just kept giving me these reasons that they couldn't see my mom, so I sat back down. And as I'm sitting there, I'm watching people come, and they're being taken in to be seen by the doctor.

What I realized is that everyone they took in was white.

We sat there for a long time. At about 9:30, they finally called my mom, and they put her in a treatment room. I felt better, as she was able to lie down. She still had the paper towel, trying to keep from vomiting. I thought,

Thank God, you know. The nurse came in and said, "We need to take your mom outside and put her in a wheelchair, because we have another gentleman who needs to see the doctor."

"No!" I insisted. "My mom's been here since two. You need to see her now!"

They went ahead and started getting her up. Oh my goodness, she vomited, and it seemed like that entire treatment room was full of blood. At that point, all the doctors and nurses, everybody was coming because she needed to be seen. Of course, they admitted her, she needed blood transfusions, so they took her to the fifth floor.

I was really livid. When we got up to the fifth floor, I heard all this laughter coming from one of the treatment rooms. The doctors and nurses had gone to the treatment room with my mom, the fifth-floor treatment room, and she was getting transfusions. I thought, *Oh, that's my mom*, cause that's the way she was. She could always make you laugh no matter what was going on. I felt a little bit better. It was very late, and they admitted her to room 501. The doctor came out and said, "You guys need to go home and get some rest. We'll call you if something happens."

I didn't want to go home. I wanted to go up to my mom. I wanted to say I love you. I wanted to give her a hug because we were not a family who did that. I didn't even remember ever saying I love you to my mom. But I couldn't, because the doctor would not let us go in. Doctors and nurses were all around the bed, and they were admitting her, and, you know, I really wanted to go and hug her, but we obeyed the doctor and just left.

They called us very early the next morning and said that she was critical and we needed to get up there. So, we went. I still wanted to get to my mom, but I couldn't because everybody was around—the doctors, nurses, they were around her bed, doing things. They said they were trying to get her ready for surgery. When they brought her out, taking her down to the second floor for surgery, I saw a glimpse of my mom's face. And this has never left me. Her eyes were swollen and there were tears in her eyes, and I still could not get to her. The doctor said I would see her when surgery was over.

We waited a long time on the second floor. The next thing we knew, the doctor came out of surgery and said, "We're sorry, but your mom didn't make it."

I was so angry. I was a teenager at that time, so I really felt like this hospital killed my mom. That's all I could think about. *You killed my mom.* I was screaming at them, "You should have seen her sooner, you could have brought her in and saved her life."

My mother's death was the main reason I wanted to continue in the civil rights movement. Because how in the world can people treat someone that way just because of the color of their skin? Today I'm still involved, and I bring Freedom Riders here for Black History Month or MLK

Day to keep this history alive. I have an organization, Dr. Bowie's Barbara Collins Bowie Scholarship Foundation, and we honor them all for what they did. Because they're the reason that we are able to do all things together as one.

I didn't think of myself as a Freedom Rider until my brother validated it for me on his dying bed. He said that the sit-ins and protests were just as important as the bus rides and going to the prison. It took all of that to get us to where we are today. I want to continue helping us learn how to bring peace and equality and justice to our lives and for our kids to know this history.

Oreo

NORMA ELIA CANTÚ

En el barrio han cambiado las cosas. Things change as they must. It used to be that dogs could come and go and be independent, if they so chose. Or they could attach themselves to homes where they were treated well. Fed. Bathed. Sometimes even given the required shots and vaccines. But not now. Now, a dog has to have a home. A leash. A plan. *Y así le tocó a Oreo*, an independent and self-sufficient dog that loved to roam all over the barrio. *Al principio*, she was a bit shy and hesitant to just go right into people's yards and lie there in the morning sun after having been fed in another home. *Pero con el tiempo*, it became easier, as things usually are after one keeps doing the same old, same old. Although she was still wary.

Especially, *después del incidente con la perrera*. Yes. Things changed a bit after that incident. No one remembers who it was—or perhaps no one knew—but someone called animal control on Oreo. Must've been *la gorda de enfrente*, people would whisper when the question came up in midmorning *pláticas* over a *cafecito*.

Because she roamed as she pleased, Oreo knew what happened in every single home in a five-block area. She was a kind of sentinel, watchful and alert. She knew the secrets and recognized each and every household's idiosyncrasies. The way the Valdez kids were so dumb they even obeyed their mother when she called them to spank them. The other kids just ran off and could not be caught if their mother called threateningly, *chancla* in hand. Oreo knew about the couple who didn't have kids and enjoyed their afternoon siesta while they watched *Jeopardy*. She stayed away from the Pérez house when the father came in drunk from the cantina demanding supper. Knew not to stay away too long from the old woman who lived alone and who was always out in the garden with her pruning shears or watering the *romero*, the yerba buena, and the roses, hibiscus, and seasonal flowers galore.

Yes, Oreo roamed the streets, usually alone, and came and went everywhere as she pleased. Other dogs wanted her to join their pack and hung around enticing her, but she would have none of it, preferring to stay alone. However, I am telling you the story about Oreo, and not the other dogs, although they, too, had a history and a life. For a while, as a pup, Oreo had a home; she stuck by the same family for almost three years. It had been almost by accident that she found that home. Oreo barely remembered how Lichita, one of the Soliz children, rescued her as some other kids were teasing and torturing her and her siblings. She became Lichita's dog; that lasted until the Soliz family moved and left her in the care of the Paredes family. But they were not as attentive and forgot to set out food or water, so she moved on.

She loved the freedom. She did as she pleased. Bark, jump, beg—whatever she wanted, whenever she wanted. Of course, there were drawbacks: no sure feeding time, no indoor mat to sleep on, no nice warm spot at night when it was dark. But back to the story of the *perrera* that taught her a lesson she didn't soon forget. That afternoon, *llegaron en el van con la jaula,* the cage that held other dogs, to haul her off to the place where strays are taken. *A veces* even the legal dogs, those that have been registered and vaccinated, even they end up *en ese lugar, esperando* against hope to be rescued. *Pero la pobre* Oreo didn't know that most times, no one comes to the rescue and off they go to certain death. She was actually excited when the two men approached her and scratched her behind her right ear, the way she liked. She came to them with her tail wagging and her ears droopy so they would not be scared and went along for the ride. But as soon as they arrived at the shelter, she realized that it had been a mistake; she should have bared her teeth and run away. *¡Si hubiera sabido!*

How the neighborhood missed her! So much so that Pati and Chole, two of the barrio women, pooled their money and asked for contributions to retrieve her. My mother put in her five dollars, expressing disgust at how someone had dared do this heinous thing. Everyone contributed, even the Anglo woman who was married to a Mejicano and rarely left her double-wide, and *la comadre* Tencha, who had so many kids it was a miracle she had any money to contribute to the cause. Everyone gave, even the woman who lived alone. Even the Paredes family—although they kept insisting that Oreo was not technically their dog, lest someone expect them to foot the bill for the release: *¡Eso se saca por andar sola, de andariega!* They claimed that her family had moved away and she had been left alone again. No one argued. They all felt that Oreo belonged to them collectively.

Oreo had been alone before. Once. A long time ago in Chicago before the move, as a young pup. Her family, los Sendejo, had picked her out from a litter that a neighbor's dog owned. When they moved to Texas, Oreo moved too—they brought her and her two siblings. *De vez en cuando*, she would have dreams about the long road trip and about the whole family nervous and excited and scared. She too was nervous and excited and scared. That was how it had been. And after a very long trip, finally they arrived in Laredo and rented the old house *en el barrio* Las Cruces; Oreo scoped it out and made friends with the other dogs in the neighborhood. The family settled in, and Oreo liked to lie out under the *nogal* in the shade on hot afternoons. She missed the crisp, cool Midwest weather, but she soon adjusted to the new world that was Laredo.

Pero it didn't last. The father started drinking. The children were not doing well in school, and the mother had two jobs trying to keep it all together. Finally, the mother had enough and took the children and went back to Chicago to be with her mother. And there was no way Oreo and her siblings could come with them. The kids cried and the mother's heart broke yet again as they left Laredo on the van with other passengers all heading to Chicago; hardly anyone traveled by bus anymore. Vans were safer and way faster. And if you got a good driver, it was a pleasant trip. Oreo missed her family and was thinking of trying her luck and following that van to her old home, until Lichita rescued her from the mean kids. She felt she owed it to Lichita to stay with her.

The memory of Oreo's Chicago family is quickly fading because you know what? She is now a respectable member of the Pérez family. After the rescue from the pound, they took her in. Gave her her shots and put a leash on her. She even goes on car rides—her head out the window, she bares her teeth to the wind, wind that caresses her ears, feels like she's flying. What a life! Even dogs have a life story, you know! And this one isn't too bad. *La pobre* Oreo, people used to say. Now they say ¡*Mirala! Parece reina, la Oreo.* And so it is: she is a queen; her subjects, her family. She cherishes her memories of being homeless but happy. Memories of having children who loved her. Memories of old *viejitas* who shared their meager meals with her. Memories of how in her youth she chased cars roaring by, not quite knowing what she would do if she ever caught one. But now, the barrio folks exclaim, *Mira la Oreo,* there she goes, smiling and feeling like a queen! *Así es la vida. ¡Una vida de perro!*

My Mother Was Thinking of Me

KELLY GREY CARLISLE

Imagine: it's two in the morning in the OB ward. My first child, Milly, is twenty-seven hours old. Our room is dark, and light filters in from the hallway to make a dim twilight around the bassinet and bed. My husband, too long for the creaking recliner, has gone home for a good night's sleep. It's our first time alone together, and our room is perfectly quiet. She's just finished nursing, and her sleeping body lies between my breasts. I'm just getting used to the little sounds she makes, little gurgles and sighs. I can barely feel the weight of her six pounds, but I can feel her warmth. I can feel the soft puff of her breath, the tiny twitch of the little fist. I'm so full of love for this little creature, barely human. So full of love that it overflows in tears that meander down my cheeks.

I wasn't this sentimental during my pregnancy. There was seldom any sighing over tiny pink socks in stores. There were no letters written to my daughter in utero as my pregnancy book suggested. On most days, I had to remember to talk to her. I had to remember to tell her I loved her. I wasn't sure that I actually did. But on this night, there is no doubt about my love. I would do anything, give anything, for her and for her happiness. I love her with every part of my being. Every humble cell, every higher thought. And it's because of this—this flood of love—that I finally know for sure that my own mother loved me.

All my life, I've wondered what my mother was like. I don't know much about her, so sometimes I take the facts that I do know and spin a story with them. I imagine her in the months before her death, maybe on the day she finally went to the clinic. It was 1976 in Los Angeles. She was twenty-three years old. My dad was in jail. Her parents weren't talking to her. She probably went to the clinic alone. I know these things, but I make up the part about the waiting room. I imagine men and women sitting in hard plastic chairs, rustling magazines and talking to each other in hushed voices. The little boy, five or six, running through the aisles who stops and stares when he comes to my mom. And maybe, for the first time that day, she felt self-conscious about her frayed jeans and her stained T-shirt, her greasy hair. She waits a very long time, and then she's taken into a little room where they give her a test, and then she waits some more. She already knows what the results will be, but someone told her that if she takes the test, she can get some money for the baby. But that's not why she'll keep it, for the money.

When the doctor comes in, he says she's pregnant. He tells her they don't do abortions there; she'll have to go somewhere else. He says there are many groups that will make it possible for her to bring the baby to term, but if she's just going to drink or do drugs or whatever, she might as well get an abortion. She stares at the dull metal of his stethoscope and wonders why he thinks she doesn't know this already. He asks her if she has any family. She says yes, and then she says nothing more. She already asked her dad for help. He said no. I know this for sure—in fact, he said, "You've really fucked up now, haven't you?" It was their last conversation.

That night, before she went to sleep, wherever it was she slept in those days, I imagine that my mother thought of her unborn child the way I often thought of my unborn child when I was pregnant. Perhaps she imagined that dark world inside her. Her little girl—she'd always known it was a little girl—floating in a shaded pool, the cord keeping her from floating off into the darkness. She closed her eyes and made a little promise that she'd look after her. She wanted to do right by her little girl, whom she'd already named, and whom she'd already, long ago, decided to keep.

Three weeks after she gave birth to me, my mother left me in a motel room in Hollywood. She laid me in a dresser drawer because she didn't have a cradle. She nestled me between some T-shirts and socks and tucked a baby blanket around me. She went out to turn a trick. We needed money for rent, food, and quite possibly for drugs. Her strangled body was found the next morning on a hillside. She'd been beaten so badly her face was unrecognizable. Her case has never been solved.

I know these things from police reports and conversations with cold case detectives, but I imagine the stuff I can't get from reports. For instance: I like to think that she kissed me before she walked off into that dark night. I like to think that she loved me, that I made her happy.

Tonight, in this hospital room, I imagine my mother nursing me and holding me afterward. When I feel Milly's breath against my chest, I know exactly how my mother felt the night I was born. I know that she loved me with every part of herself, every humble cell, every higher thought.

Sometimes I wonder who was in the hospital room with her. Surely not my father, whom I've never met. Not her parents. She was alone.

Were the nurses kind when they told her to push, or did they look at her with cold eyes when they said, "It's a girl," and smiled tightly? There were no flowers, no cards or gifts in my mom's hospital room. There was nothing. Just her own warm clothes folded neatly on a chair.

My mother got pregnant three years after *Roe v. Wade.* She was broke. She was alone. She'd never even really had a family. I've often wondered why she kept me. And now, in the hospital room, holding my child, I think the answer was just that she wanted to start a family. She wanted a baby. She wanted not to be alone; she wanted someone to love. And I think now how she only had three weeks of this. This, holding a baby in your arms, those little gurgles and sighs, those whispers of smiles and sleep. Only three weeks of this pure, pure love. I cry at the thought of only having three weeks.

All my life, I thought that her killer's greatest crime was taking my mother away from me, but now, holding my baby, I know that that's not true. The true crime was taking a mother away from her baby. It was taking her away from the love that she had so bravely fashioned for herself. It was crushing it with the brutal force of blunt fists and tight rope. And I know this now, I know what my mother was thinking right before she died.

In her last shudders and spasms, in that terrible moment before she blacked out—when she knew that she wasn't going to get away—my mother thought about her baby girl. My mother thought about me.

Are You Out There?

CARY CLACK

Mistakes aren't intentional. By definition, a mistake is something taken in error: poor judgment, a bad choice. The certainty that something is a mistake isn't known until after the fact. So, there's a question mark next to the big mistake I'll speak of because I don't know how it turned out after the fact.

About twenty-five years ago, on a Sunday night, I was at home. I was dozing off on the living room couch when I heard footsteps running up the porch followed by banging on the metal screen door and a woman's voice yelling, "Help me, please help me."

Startled out of my sleep, my mind started trying to associate that voice with any of the women in my life. I stumbled across the room, switched on the porch light, and opened the front door just enough to see out. Banging on the screen door was a young woman, or girl, maybe eighteen or nineteen years old. She was African American, her brown face glazed with perspiration and maybe tears. She was short, a little stocky, and the gray sweatshirt she wore had grass stains, as did her red jeans. She was clutching the screen's protective bars with her left hand while banging on the door with her right hand. When she saw me, she blurted out, "Please, mister, please help me."

I was almost shouting as I asked her, "What? What's wrong? What's going on?"

She quickly looked behind her and then back at me. "They're—they're after me. They're going to hurt me. Please help me, mister!"

"Who's after you?"

"These—these two girls. They say I've been messing with their boyfriends, trying to get close with them, and they say they're going to kick my ass. They've been chasing me for two blocks. I ain't done nothing! Don't let them get me!"

Her voice was desperate. Through the screen door, I couldn't see or hear anyone else outside. I asked her what her name was.

"My name's Katie," she said. "I don't have anywhere to go. Please let me in. Don't let them get me!"

By this time I'd fully opened the door, but the screen door was still locked. I said, "Katie, I—I don't see anyone else. Where are they?"

"Mister, I ain't lying," she said indignantly. "They're after me. Please let me in!"

I kind of felt as if she were telling the truth, but I was unsure—and, yes, I was afraid. I didn't know if she was part of a con. Maybe she had accomplices out there lurking in the shadows.

I told her I would call the police for her.

"Do you have to?" she asked.

"*Yes*, if you're in trouble and someone's trying to hurt you, maybe the police can help. Stay here on the porch, I'll call them and come right back and talk to you."

She nodded her head slowly and sadly and sat down on the top porch step, sobbing while I closed the door halfway to go call the police. This was long before I had a cell phone, and when the landline still had a cord, so I couldn't make the phone call while watching her at the door. I was on the phone with the police dispatcher for no more than three minutes.

When I went back to the door, Katie was gone. Twice I called her name, and twice there was no answer. I opened the screen door, went out to the sidewalk, and looked up and down the street, but I didn't see her or anyone else. I wanted to ask my neighbors if they had seen or heard anything, but none of them were outside.

I was going inside the house when the police car drove up. I explained to him what had happened. He said he would drive around the neighborhood and let me know if he saw or came across anything. I went back into the house, and that was it. I sat down and thought about what had just happened, feeling a growing sense of unease. Over the next few days, I paid closer attention to the news in case there was a story involving a young woman who might have been Katie, but I never read or saw anything like that.

If Katie was telling the truth and was in distress, my big mistake was not responding to that distress, for allowing my fears to keep me from helping someone. On the other hand, there are so many things that can go wrong in letting a stranger, a teenage girl, into your home, especially if she is running a con. It's possible I could be telling you now that my big mistake was allowing a stranger into my house.

And so the question mark looms.

The story of the Good Samaritan is about having the courage to help others, even if it puts you at risk. His decision proved to not be a mistake, a certainty that I—the reluctant, uncertain Samaritan—will never have when it comes to Katie.

To be honest, if what happened twenty-five years ago was to happen tonight, I don't have the certainty that my decision would be different. I just don't know.

I do know that all these years later, when I think back to that night, I end up thinking to myself, *Katie, where are you? Are you out there?*

Puro San Antonio

JESS ELIZARRARAS

San Antonio was recently ranked as one of the top five friendliest cities in America by something called homes .com. Those polls are usually bullshit. They're created by whatever start-up, rideshare, or real estate company made them, and that's what they use to market themselves. Because, of course, news media outlets like the one I work for pick them up and put them online. But San Antonians puffed their chests. They clapped. They smiled broadly, they patted themselves on the back. Of course, we're the friendliest, *yes*. Have you been to the Alamo yet? Have you been by Market Square? Have you tried all of the nineteen restaurants at the Pearl? Have you had the puffy tacos at *insert your favorite Tex-Mex restaurant name here*? But for this eighteen-year-old Rio Grande Valley transplant, San Antonio was anything but friendly.

I moved here to get a taste of the big city. I'm from Brownsville, and back then—as well as now—Brownsville was synonymous with immigration and family separation. I left in 2004 when there were 164,000 people, and 163,000 of them looked just like me. They were *mi gente*; they spoke my language, they didn't have to pay for breakfast or lunch at school, they knew their way around a flea market—or *pulgas*, as we liked to call them, because we didn't really go to Target until the mid-2000s. And most of them were first- or second-generation immigrants like me and my family, and they still made almost weekly visits across *el puente*—some of us got our braces done there.

When I left, I wanted to experience it all. I wanted to make my mark. But have you heard the phrase "small fish, big pond"? I was a guppy in every sense of the word. I started at the University of Texas at San Antonio that fall and made a handful of friends, but I mostly stuck to what I knew. If you've ever been to UTSA's main campus, it's suburban at best. It didn't help that I didn't have a car, so no exploring, because I wasn't going to take the VIA bus and get lost for an hour and a half. UTSA was very much a commuter campus, and back then we used to do this fun thing where everyone fought *Hunger Games*–style for that sweet, sweet parking space like a mile away from our next class. And then on the way back, someone would follow your car, creeping slowly. We called it sharking. There wasn't a group of friends hanging out at the student center. The football team—go, Runners!—were but a glimmer in the school administration's eyes.

So when I did start making friends, I kind of stuck out. I didn't really blend in with a good portion of the sororities that were made up of blond, blue-eyed people. I spoke fluent Spanish, and it turns out I had an accent I wasn't aware of. Spanish was what we spoke at home, the minute I got inside the house—I still can't speak to my mom in English. It wasn't easy. I still did that Valley girl thing—do you guys know what I'm talking about? The tongue click. And even when I finally got wheels, there was no way I was going on the highway. There was no way I was going inside Loop 410. Coming from a one-highway town, I didn't really understand—410, I-10, I-35, 1604, 281, 151, 90—like, what? And honestly, I don't think most San Antonians get it either.

Eventually, in my third year, I switched my major—as one does. I decided I wanted to be a journalist. As a young reporter, I was finding stories across campus, and when my assignments, internships, and later jobs brought me downtown, I started to learn about a whole new *San Anto* that I'm still getting to know. I learned about Fiesta—though I didn't understand cascarones or medals. I had my first puffy taco from Ray's, of course, on Nineteenth Street. And I learned more about the city. I learned about its neighborhoods, its traditions, its fabrics.

With my alienist storytelling, I was supposed to blend in and absorb and document and report back, but when you come down here you have a whole new set of people to blend in with, and I think that was a harder portion for me. It was a culture shock. It was the *puro* vetting process. Or as my friend puts it, the *puro* pissing contest.

For those not familiar, *puro* is a sense of ownership, a sense of place, and here it means knowing everything in and out about San Anto, which I didn't. Trying to cover that new part of the city was difficult. It was like Jennifer Lopez or Edward James Olmos says in the movie *Selena*, being Mexican American is hard. You have to be twice as perfect as everyone else. You have to be more Mexican than the Mexicans, and at the same time you have to prove to the Americans how American you are. It's exhausting. In San Anto, I had to prove how Mexican I was, how American I was, and how *puro* I was. All while losing parts of my native tongue and losing my connection with the border.

In San Anto, my Spanish has faded because I have so few people to practice it with, and now I struggle for words with my parents on the phone. But I have *papel picado* at the house, and I wear embroidered shirts. I didn't go to Fox Tech or Brack or Harlandale or Jeff, but I probably watched the same telenovelas those kids did growing up. I have a Hot Cheetos complex, which means that as a food writer, I know they're not good for me but I'm still going to drown them in Ricos cheese when no one's around.

Like other Valley or border town natives, I still long for "real tacos," the ones that come in a half dozen and are piled high with queso fresco. Or the gas station tacos from Stripes that fueled half of my high school shenanigans. I'm still kind of an alien on purpose now. But I'm stalking the food in San Antonio that's so quickly changing. We're not just Tex-Mex anymore. I'm trying to make those "exotic" ingredients less alien. Because they're not. But at least now I can point you in the direction of Market Square and tell you where to eat a puffy taco.

I Smell Gas

GEORGIA ERCK

I worry that I might turn into my mother or, worse, my father. My mother was a writer and had agoraphobia, fear of open places. She couldn't drive on the expressway or go to the mall. My sisters and I did most of the grocery shopping because the shiny linoleum floors at Handy Andy made her feel like she would faint.

She worried about everything. "I smell gas. Do you smell it?"

"No," I'd say.

My sister would come in the room.

"Do you smell gas?" Mom would ask again.

"No, ma'am."

My dad would come home from work.

"Jimmy, I think we have a gas leak."

"Oh, hell, Phyllis. Quit being so goddamn spastic."

"Well, whatever you do, don't light your cigar or we'll all blow up!"

When I was eleven, my sisters drove me to Mr. W Fireworks, and I saw something called cigarette loads, which gave me a great idea. My mom smoked Salem Lights 100s. I went home, got a pack off the kitchen counter, took out

the cigarettes, and pushed the load into the brown to-
bacco end. Then I put the cigarettes back in the pack and
waited. I waited for two days. I even forgot about it until
that night while I was watching *Barnaby Jones* in the living room with my dad. We heard a *pow!* and then Mom
screaming, "Jimmy! Ooh, Jimmy!"

I knew right away what had happened. She always
leaned over and lit her cigarettes over our gas stove.

My dad and I raced into the kitchen. My mom was
slumped over the butcher block, the end of her cigarette
blown up like a pom-pom. "Jimmy! The stove exploded! I
told you we have a gas leak!"

"Calm down, Phyllis," he said. I could tell he was onto
me, even before I denied it. Then when I did, I got in huge
trouble for lying.

As an adult, I was walking down my street once and
thought, *Oh, no, I smell gas. Maybe I should call someone.
What if someone drives by and tosses a cigarette out the
window? Half the block will explode.* Then I said out loud,
"Shut up, Phyllis!"

My dad was the opposite of my mother. He wanted
every day to be a party, with him as the honoree. He was
notorious for going onstage at weddings and shows and
taking the microphone away from people to do his own
bit. He even did it to Bob Hope once.

I don't know. Maybe we do become our parents. Look
at me, a scared-shitless writer. I do know one thing. Both

my parents died recently, and now that they're gone, I'd do just about anything to get them back.

After my mom died, I went to her best friend to figure out how to be on the planet without a mother. I sat down with Mrs. Tassos at her kitchen table, like we'd done for so many years. Nothing had changed. Everything was the same, except my mother wasn't there with her gin martini. So, everything was different. I was telling Mrs. T how devastated I was when I got the call that my mom had died—unexpectedly, while I was in another country—and her son came in and interrupted us. He started hugging me like Greek people do, and I tried to get back to my story, but then Mrs. T interrupted me.

"Danny, where are the ribs?" she said.

"Sorry. They ran out of ribs today."

"Then what are we supposed to have for supper?"

I looked at him and back at her. I was thinking, *Hello . . . I'm really sad here*, but they needed to figure out their dinner plan. I knew they both loved my mom, but they had moved on.

A few months ago, I stopped by a store to find a baby present for my grandnephew that my niece and her wife are fostering to adopt. I went in and started talking to the lady behind the counter. We talked about Día de Los Muertos and the painted skulls she sells, and we somehow wound up talking about Donald Trump, how he'd thrown paper towels at a crowd of hurricane survivors in Puerto Rico as if to say, "I'm here to help. Here, go on and get started without me." We both shook our heads.

"I don't know," I said. "The world is in a really weird place right now."

"The hairs just stood up on my arm when you said that!" she said.

"Why?"

"I don't know. I guess because of all the stuff that's going on, we just have to do our best to get through it. Actually...my son died recently," she said. "That's him, over there in the corner."

There was a beautiful shrine with a picture of her adult son in the center. It made me think of my own adult son.

"That's terrible," I said. "I'm so sorry."

"No, it's okay. He was sick. A lot. He was epileptic. He had seizures every day. In the end, he was having like forty seizures a day."

"That must've been so hard on both of you."

"It was. I worried about him all the time. I tried to prepare him. I'm in my sixties; his father is seventy-two. I told him, 'I won't be around forever. Someday you'll be here without me.' He didn't understand. So, I said, 'It's like this. You know how I'm here right now talking to you?'

'Yeah.' Then I went in the next room behind the wall.

'You think I'm still here?'

'Yeah.'

'It's like that. I'll still be with you. You just won't be able to see me anymore.' And you know what the strange thing is? All that time I thought I was preparing him for the day I wouldn't be here, and really, I was being prepared for the day he would die. It's been hard, but he's free now. I text my other kids every month on the day and say, 'He hasn't had a seizure in five months. He's seizure-free. He's at peace.' And I'm free. I can do all the things I couldn't all those years I was taking care of him. He wanted that for me. I'm going to start traveling and getting to know the women who make the things I've sold in the store."

It made me think of how, after my mom died, I decided to pretend heaven was just another city she had moved to so I wouldn't miss her so much. Like death was just a change of address and someday I'd go visit her.

The woman started folding the onesie I was buying, which had *Todos somos primos* printed on the front. "That means 'We're all cousins,' right?" I asked.

"Well, literally. But really it means 'We're all connected. We're all family.' I'm sorry. You're a customer. I don't know why I just told you about my son."

"No, I'm so glad you did. The story about your son and some things my mom's best friend said are starting to make sense."

I realized that when someone we love dies, we're still alive, even though it doesn't feel like it half the time. We have to continue on without them because the world doesn't stop and wait for anyone, even if there's a death in the family. When your son or your mother or your father dies, somebody's still got to buy the ribs.

The Vegetarian with Swine Flu

TIFFANY FARIAS-SOKOLOSKI

Ever since I can remember, I've wanted to travel the world. I am the youngest of three girls, I am Latina, and I grew up in McAllen, Texas. Growing up, my life was a bubble that was the Rio Grande Valley. In fact, my mom would shoot me incredulous looks anytime I talked about wanting to travel anywhere beyond San Antonio. When she found out I had been accepted to teach abroad in Thailand, she was not happy!

The conversation went a little like this: "Mom, guess what, I'm going to be in Thailand for three weeks!" Her response was, "Thailand! You can teach here! Why would you go to Thailand when you can teach here? What if something happens, ¿*entonces qué*?" As one can imagine, my decision to go left my mom uneasy, but I was not about to let her get in the way of my dream to travel the world. I was proud of making a decision for myself. I knew this trip would be the start of not only a new adventure but a pathway to new understandings and ways of being. A few weeks later, I packed my bags and headed to my teaching assignment in Thailand.

After about a thirty-two-hour flight, we landed in Bangkok. I was feeling pretty dizzy, just not feeling well at all. *This must be jet lag*, I thought. *Certainly it's jet lag.* I figured it was something I could sleep away.

That first day was full of excursions, like going on a boat ride, visiting temples, leisurely walks through the city, and meeting people. It was all so entertaining, but something continued to not sit right with me. Each place we visited carried with it an awful, overwhelming smell. I mean, no joke, I thought I was going to puke at every place we visited. Picture this: I'm with a group of a dozen people. We go to a temple, everybody's pointing out these awesome things, and there I am, like, "Oh, that's—*humph.*" And then on a boat ride, we get in the boat—*humph*. And how can I forget meeting people? When they put their hand out to shake mine, there I was trying hard not to puke on them. Everybody was so patient and so nice, and they kept telling me things like, "Don't worry. It happens to the best of us. What you're experiencing is jet lag, so don't worry about it." Naturally, I thought to myself, *Jet lag sucks!*

That night my roommate Danica and I got absolutely no sleep. I had a terrible cough. It sounded like a loud, angry goose. The next morning at breakfast, Danica held up the newspaper she was reading and said, "Wouldn't it be super funny if that's what you have?" She pointed out the headline, which read "H101 takes over Thailand."

"That would be hilarious! Imagine that. A vegetarian with swine flu." We both broke out in laughter and gathered our things for the trip to our teaching assignment in Trang.

We met our group at the hotel lobby, loaded our bags, and headed to the airport. The ride was quick and easy, and before I knew it I was in my assigned seat on the plane. Everything was fine until about ten minutes into the flight. I felt like my ears would explode, like the cartoon characters that shoot fire out of their ears. My bones felt like they were breaking. My body felt like it was melting from the inside out. The pain was so intense that I couldn't bear to touch my bags—even that hurt. My travel mates carried them, and my professors immediately took me to a clinic. "Whatever she has, we can't treat her here," the doctors told us. "She needs to go to a hospital."

My professors rushed me to a hospital. Once I was checked in, a nurse came to get me. I passed out as soon as I stood up. The next thing I knew I was being rolled off on a gurney. As I went in and out of consciousness, as my eyes slowly opened and closed, I heard my mom's voice telling me, "*Ay*, Tiffany, what if something happens? This is not safe! What if something happens, *¿entonces qué*?" You better not die, I told myself, because if you do Mom is going to be so mad at you!

I found myself in a room surrounded by Thai doctors and nurses. One of our Thai friends had a towel over my head, and he was telling me, "It's okay, you're going to be fine." I passed out again and woke up in a different room. This time I was alone. I tried to make sense of what was happening. I was in a hospital gown, all of my belongings were shoved in the corner, and I had one shoe on. What was happening? Could Danica have been right? Was I the vegetarian with swine flu? It took me a while, but I finally came to the realization that I was in quarantine.

The nurses were so sweet, and my host family visited me every day, leaving me gifts and sending me high fives through the window. Even locals came to visit, trying to get a glimpse of me through the window because I'd made the front-page news. This time the headline read "American Brings Disease." After about five days, I was released from the hospital. I learned that the university's president had ordered our group to return to the States.

While my first experience abroad was short-lived, I was happy to know that my mom was not mad at me, that I was able to travel abroad, and that I would have one hell of a story to share with the world.

A Science Experiment Gone Wrong

ELIZABETH FAUERSO

This is the story of a series of incidents that happened in Fairfield, Iowa, in 1986. My family and I had moved there from Malibu, California, a few years earlier, and while most people scrunch up their faces and say "My god, why?" when I frame the story this way, my sister and I were thrilled with the move.

My parents were and still are leaders in the Transcendental Meditation movement, and we moved to Fairfield so they could help start the Maharishi International University and our grade school, Maharishi School of the Age of Enlightenment. We would be reunited with many of the friends we had grown up with, roaming the Swiss Alps while our parents spent long hours meditating and studying with Maharishi in an aging hotel high on a cliff over Lake Lucerne—the one that made Wes Anderson's set for the *Grand Budapest Hotel* look as prosaic and mundane as a Holiday Inn Express.

My mother is a founding trustee of the university, and my father was head of the music department. We found

ourselves in the eclectic, brilliant, and passionately op-
timistic company of meditators from all over the world
committed to building a university and community in
Iowa based on the idea of consciousness-based education
and spiritual evolution. Our school and the university occupied the stately campus of the defunct Parsons College,
a private school for rich flunk-outs that lost its accredita-
tion. So, while my description of our community may lead
some to picture a tepee-strewn commune peppered with
dashiki-clad dudes and caftan-wearing mamas, a casual
viewing of our school and community would read more
private Catholic school and bucolic small-town America.

In our elementary school, we wore uniforms, studied
the classics, put on plays by George Bernard Shaw, and
learned algebra. We also meditated twice a day, did yoga
in gym class, and had Sanskrit as a foreign-language op-
tion. All this is necessary context for the story, for little
will make sense without it.

I was mulling over my assignment to develop a project for the elementary school science fair. This was no
small task. Our school was academically rigorous, and my
class of twenty-three went on to produce multiple merit
scholars and very high achievers. I was admittedly a lib-
eral arts kid versus one drawn to the hard sciences. My
musician father and poet mother would have us sit quietly
at brunch listening to Herbie Hancock and Joni Mitch-
ell while we readied ourselves to choose our poems or

prose to read during our Sunday-morning creative time. I was also a great lover of animals, always searching for wounded birds to nurse in the wilds that surrounded our home and spending hours at the barn where my mean Appaloosa pony Cinnamon resided.

As such, my science fair project had a kind of poetic, loose feel from its inception. I acquired two groups of ten mice and placed them in two distinct environments. Group one, dubbed the Plebeians by me and my family, would lead the relatively mundane lives of normal mice, eating store-bought food and drinking tap water from their dispenser. Group two, the Ayurvedans, would follow the health practices of the ancient principles of Ayurveda (holistic medicine) and Gandharva veda (traditional Indian music) that, combined, are supposed to increase coherence, health, and well-being.

One of the primary principles of Ayurveda is the idea of different body types or doshas: *pitta* (fire), *vata* (wind), and *kapha* (earth/water). When your dosha is out of balance, that dosha's characteristics show up as health problems. I made the determination that mice are vata deranged—like too much wind, possessing the characteristics of hyperactivity, restlessness, and lack of focus—and devised an experiment to test the efficacy of Ayurvedic treatments for vata imbalance. I would play Gandharva veda and give vata tea meant to soothe the windblown, vata-imbalanced mice.

It is important to note that when I selected the twenty mice at the pet store, I did little to confirm the teenage clerk's claim that they had been segregated by gender. The two groups of ten quickly became two groups of twenty, then thirty, then forty. The project's dependence on the comparison with the control group and thus any scientific validity were completely destroyed, but with the dreamy sounds of Mose Allison lulling me into poetic submission, I forged ahead, unchecked by reason or scientific method.

Upon returning home from school one day, I encountered the first piece of evidence pointing to the project's catastrophic breakdown. A dead mouse lay gutted on the steps inside the mudroom. Then another, and another, and another. A relatively straight line of disemboweled mice led down the hall, past the dining room, living room, and kitchen, down the stairs to the basement. One mouse per stair, through the playroom and into the storage rooms where the experiment was taking place. In the hall connecting the Plebeians and the Ayurvedans we found our Siamese cat, Cheeto, his long black tail with a kink at the end waving wildly back and forth, his tan muzzle smeared with blood, a mouse clutched in each paw. His blue eyes were wide and savage, looking much like Marlon Brando at the end of *Apocalypse Now* repeating, "the horror, the horror."

My mother, sister, and I were all screaming—and so overwhelmed by the true horror of the scene that we ran upstairs to call my father so he could apprehend this wild beast that bore so little resemblance to our lazy, docile house cat. Someone, and we will never know who, had left the door to the basement open. Many lives were lost, close to seventy. The crew of eighty mice, most born in our home, had been culled to less than ten terrified survivors.

I spent the night trying to nurse wounded subjects back to health but fell asleep and woke up with a dead mouse in each hand.

We were faced with another inflection point: the experiment was destroyed, there was no way forward with anything close to a valid scientific outcome, and yet we proceeded. We called the Fairfield pet shop to inquire about more mice, and the same young man who had supposedly separated the mice by sex reminded us that we had already bought all the mice. He recommended that we call the pet shop in neighboring Ottumwa.

For those of you not familiar with Ottumwa, Iowa, let me set the stage. It is a relatively small town nestled between the muddy Ottumwa River and a vast expanse of slaughterhouses and meatpacking plants. It's rumored that Al Capone had a hideout there, and the community, as you can imagine, was permeated with a palpable brutality and the literal stench of death. Perfect place to get replacement mice for the science fair you are trying to cheat your way through.

At the Ottumwa pet store, we found the mice, like most residents of the town, to be bigger than the rest of us. They were bruisers, possessing none of the discreet charms of the dainty mice I had started with, which seemed well suited for Beatrix Potter–style anthropomorphization. The store only had eight, so we took them all. When we returned home with the paper bags full of frantic bully mice, we dropped four in the Plebeian and four in the Ayurvedan aquariums. Almost immediately the Ottumwans started aggressing on the survivors. "Maybe they just need a few minutes to get used to each other," we said.

But after checking on them an hour later and seeing that the Ottumwans had ripped the hair off the backs of some of the survivors, I felt I had no choice but to throw the bullies into the snow and let them face the cruelty of the elements on their own terms.

Now I had five Plebeians and four Ayurvedans. I became so stressed that I kicked a hole through the wall next to my bed when I woke to the sound of mice scratching behind the plaster. But as the project completion date drew near, the survivors had vigorously multiplied and gotten their numbers back up to a strong twenty-five-ish per aquarium.

My final test of the Ayurvedic treatments' efficacy was to run the mice through a maze I had made with paper plates and record their times. I tried to manage the process, but the weary survivors and their too-young offspring climbed the plates and clung to the edges or frantically tried to dig their way under and out of the maze. As I sat there trying to conduct the last poorly conceived element of the project, tears streaming down my face, my mother came in, gingerly took the clipboard from my hands, and proceeded to write down fake completion times for all the subjects.

By this point our whole family had been traumatized by the project, and I believe my mother made the assessment that we could not tolerate another loss in the form of public admission of total failure.

We dutifully put together a poster board display announcing that the project had proven my hypothesis correct.

I won second prize in the science fair, and on our way to a family vacation in Hawaii we released the fifty or so mice in our friend's barn on the outskirts of town, never to admit that we were the source of his several-years-long mouse problem.

Saving History

EVERETT L. FLY

In my first semester as a graduate student in landscape architecture at the Harvard University Graduate School of Design, I was required to take a history class. It was taught by one of the world's most prominent cultural geographers and landscape historians, John Brinckerhoff Jackson. John had a very different perspective about land and landscape. He talked about the rituals, traditions, and customs different folks used, including Indigenous folks, European ethnic groups, and all other groups in between. He talked about how they left their mark on the land. The class was so big that I just sat at the back and took notes.

One of the requirements was a term paper, and as John talked through the semester, it bothered me that he said little about African Americans and what they did to help shape—and continue to shape—the American landscape. When it came time to turn in a proposal for the paper, I thought, *Here's my chance. I'm going to see if I can get this Harvard professor to think about some of the things I think about*. Most of the students' papers came back with a few comments and something like, *Okay, go ahead*. But my proposal came back with a note: "Please make an appointment to see Professor Jackson."

Since I had never talked to John face-to-face, I didn't know what to expect. I assumed he would probably tell me that my proposal was too unorthodox and I should take a more traditional topic, and that if I didn't I would be asked to leave the class. I went to his office, which was on the second floor of Old Robinson Hall, on the east end of Harvard Yard. You could look out John's window and see students crossing the quad, going to the library, or going to class—it was very intimidating. But to my surprise, John said he was really interested in my proposal to study historic African American settlements and landmarks. I explained that my family was from Nacogdoches County in Texas and that those were my roots. He said he thought this was very important and I should study it, and I could do that for my term paper, under one condition.

"If you start this," he said, "you can't come back in the middle of the paper and change to an easier topic. It's not going to be easy. There are no books, there are no anthologies, there are very few bibliographies. There are only one or two theses across the country, and they just deal with local landmarks. I want you to look as broad as you can. And I'm going to help you."

He turned to one of the teaching assistants and said, "Get Mr. Fly a rare books stack pass, and put it under my name." Within a couple of days, I had the card, which let me into the rare books collections at Harvard University.

By the time the paper was due, I'd found roughly two hundred historic African American landmarks, settlements, villages, districts, and neighborhoods. It was enough to make my point with John. It was enough to pass the class.

In fall 1976 John came back to teach the class at Harvard for what would be the last time. Within a few days, he sent one of the teaching assistants to summon me to meet with him.

"Why?" I said to the assistant. "I passed the class last year. What am I supposed to do now?"

"I don't know," he said, "but you better go because if you don't, you're not going to get out of here."

I went to meet Professor Jackson in his office. He was very glad to see me, and he said, "What did you do with that paper that you wrote last year?"

"It's somewhere in a box," I said.

"Well, I want you to continue that work," he said. "In addition, I want you to give a presentation to my graduate seminar before Thanksgiving."

"I've already got a class load," I said. "I'm taking five or six graduate-level courses. One is landscape architecture design. I'm not going to have time to do that."

"Don't worry, I'll take care of it. I'll talk to the chair of the department, I'll talk to your design professor, and we'll get it handled." John turned to the teaching assistant and said, "Get Mr. Fly another rare books stack pass."

By the time we got to November and the graduate seminar presentation, I had found about four hundred Black settlements, towns, villages, landmarks, districts, and neighborhoods across the United States. After Thanksgiving, some of the students and even the faculty began to bring me copies of articles about historic Black towns, settlements, and communities around the country where they lived. I knew at that point I had something unique.

One of the things I realize in hindsight is that John Jackson listened to me, and I listened to him. He encouraged me to take a national perspective in my work. He opened doors I could not have opened myself. Harvard's landscape architecture program is the oldest of its kind in the United States. It was established in 1901. In 1975 only four African Americans had been admitted to that program, including myself. None had finished until I received my degree in 1977. There were no Black faculty to take on this issue. At the time, the Graduate School of Design wasn't known for its focus on African American or ethnic history and what we now call environmental justice, so John Jackson stuck his neck out for me. He helped open the door and push me through.

I continued to correspond with John for the next nineteen years, until he passed away. One day in 1987 my phone rang here in San Antonio. I answered, and he said,

"Everett, this is John." That was the way he would talk. "This is John. I have something I want to tell you."

"What's on your mind?" I said.

"I want to let you know that I'm Black," he said. "In other words, I'm biracial, and I want my friends to know, and you've been such a good friend all these years. You're one of the people I wanted to tell."

John's prophecy about my work came to fruition last year when the phone rang at my house and I learned that I had received the National Humanities Medal from the president of the United States for my body of work preserving historic Black settlements.

Texas Roots

LARRY GARZA

My name is Larry Garza, and I want to tell you a story about my roots. A lot of questions come with that. What are roots? Do they begin with you and your personal story? Do they begin with your families? Or are they from your ancestors, who were cultivated from the forcible devils that made your culture, our culture?

I'm a stand-up comedian, and I've been doing comedy since the early 2000s. I want to tell you the story about a pissed-off white guy from the last show I did before the pandemic. This happened in a small Texas town called Devine when everything was starting with Covid. As you can tell, my career was skyrocketing in the stand-up world. I was performing in a privately owned Texas roadhouse, a small Hooters-meets-steak house, that sort of situation. I was paid up front, which was great, and it included dinner. I didn't want to be rude, so I ordered chicken wings—as opposed to being a dick and getting the giant porterhouse and being, you know, that guy. I brought openers with me—my friend Christopher Breakell, who can be best described as an intellectual comedian who looks like an alt-right accountant, and Freddy Treviño. Freddy is best described, I'd say, as a handicapped cholo. I know that sounds rude, but that's not a bit, that's not an act; he has a spinal disease. And totally Mexican, khaki from head to toe, he basically looks as if somebody put a gardener in a taffy puller. That was my opening act. We're having a good time.

The seating situation was typical for bar shows. The area in front of the stage was set up like a wedding ceremony, with high-top seating in the back. It was basically the mullet of table arrangements, business in the front and party in the back. Like most semiconscious audiences, everyone decided to sit in the high-tops, so there was a long row of empty seats between us and the thirty-odd people who showed up.

The show was going well. Chris did good. Freddy did good. I go onstage and start with my stereotypical Mexican humor. I'm making fun of Freddy and how twisted this pretzeled prince is. I'm making fun of Chris. I'm giving the audience what they love, the Mexican stereotype, jealous Latina wife material. I talk about my cancer and compare it to selling fruit on the side of the road. But things get a little more interesting when I start talking about Texas history.

I don't know exactly what I said, but it was a bit I've done often. It really pissed off this Foghorn Leghorn. I started to talk about the origins of the Mexican people. When I did that, Foghorn and Elmer Fudd and Yosemite

Sam got up. They'd had it. They didn't make a commotion, but they were leaving. And me, trying to save 10 percent of the audience, I asked why. Where were they going? What I could do for them to stay?

Foghorn turned around and said, "I'm tired of going to comedy shows and having to deal with politics." Now I didn't know this steak house in Devine was a beacon of political humor, but apparently it was. And Foghorn wasn't taking it. Essentially what set him off so bad was this: I talked about how to deal with racist white people on the internet.

I started by telling about the time this man came up to me and said, "I ain't racist or anything but..." We all know—any sane human being knows—that any time you hear someone start a sentence this way, it's going to be followed by something very, very racist.

He said, "I ain't racist or anything, but I think you people should go back where you came from."

To which I responded, "Seguin?"

"No, no, no," the man said, apologetically. "I don't mean where you came from, I mean where your ancestors came from."

And I went, "Oh. You mean Seguin?"

Because we never left. We just stayed in the Seguin area while different cultures tried to take over the land we know now as Texas but that was always just land to us. We stood around, and our eye color changed, and our skin tone lightened. We started off as Indigenous people, and then Spaniards came, and Spaniards are from what continent? Europe. Who lives in Europe? White people. So, these white people came and turned my great, great, great-grandma Xochi Naqualate into Olivia Rodriguez, and then she started to speak Spanish. Spanish wasn't our native tongue, but we were forced to speak it, just like those Spaniards forced themselves on Xochi, creating an entire race of mestizos.

We didn't just lay down and take it. We created an entire culture and became the Republic of Mexico, and we built this empire, strong and proud, as much as we could, until these other Europeans came over seeking religious asylum.

Can you imagine that? People coming over because the country they lived in sucked? But these white people had bluer eyes. We know the story, right? It was the Alamo. It was Sam Houston and David Bowie and "Stone Cold" Steve Austin. I didn't pay close attention, but I just said, "Look. Let's not blame people for speaking Spanish in a country that's made of immigrants."

But Foghorn wasn't going to sit there and let some wetback use a Texas rattlesnake's name in vain. He was pissed, and he let me know. He aggressively stood there, and people tried to stop him, and it was an awkward situation. It wasn't the first time I've dealt with a heckler, let alone someone running up to the stage, because if I can dish it out, I can take it. So, I told them, let him speak.

"I'm tired of white people being persecuted," he said. "Every time I go to a comedy show, white people are being made fun of. Why is it okay for you to use the term 'white devil'?" Which I never did. I guess it was the white guilt inside him, the white devil. Why could I use a term like "white devil," he wanted to know, but he couldn't use any racial slurs?

I was like, you can use all the racial slurs you want, dude, who's stopping you?

And a woman—my white knight—said, "I don't mind it if he calls us white devils. Just sit down and enjoy the show. You need to have more dignity than that."

"Look," I said. "I have just one question for you. Obviously, you're deeply offended by the racial stereotypes of white people I put out. But you're totally okay with me ragging on a handicapped man for the first ten minutes of my set, is that correct?"

"You don't understand," he said. "I'm more Mexican than you are."

"How's that?"

"I married a Mexican, and my kids are half Mexican."

"Oh," I said. "Well, that's exactly what happened to my great, great, great-grandma Xochi."

I got more of a gasp than a laugh. Yosemite Sam and Elmer Fudd had to grab Foghorn and lead him out of the Looney Tune we created, and my show ended just like it began—awkwardly.

I often ask myself if I would have done things differently if I'd known this would be the last show I'd do before the pandemic. The last live show I would ever headline. Maybe I would have left well enough alone. Should I have let him walk away? I definitely should have ordered a porterhouse steak.

The Beatdown That Wasn't

LORENZO GOMEZ III

This story is about a hustle I ran when I was in middle school. It's actually more of a street hustle—the type of hustle you'd see in a prison documentary or *Lord of the Flies*—so I hope I don't traumatize you too much.

I went to school at Tafolla on the West Side. A little context for you: Tafolla is in the poorest zip code in Bexar County and arguably one of the poorest zip codes in the country. When I was as a sixth-grader there in 1993, San Antonio was in the middle of a ten-year surge in gang violence. It was at its highest level in the city's history. The year I got to seventh grade, San Antonio reached its highest level of drive-by shootings. There were about three drive-by shootings every day that year, and my neighborhood was the second hottest spot for drive-bys. So, as a twelve- or thirteen-year-old, I was kind of scared all the time. By eighth grade, I was really afraid.

The main thing I had to be afraid of at Tafolla was gangs. Three main gangs ran the school. The first gang was called the NDs, and I still don't know what that stands for. I think it had something to do with Notre Dame, but a friend once said he thought it stood for no dads, which is really depressing, and I hope it's not true. These were the biggest, baddest *vatos* in the school. They'd all flunked, like, three grades, so they were adults masquerading as middle school kids. They didn't really cause any trouble—it was like middle school was beneath them. They did all of their badness outside of school, so I didn't really worry about them too much.

The second gang was run by this guy Raymond. They didn't really have a name—it was just his crew. I met him on my first day in gym class, and he said, "Hey, my name is Raymond." The next thing he said was, "I'm part of the junior Mexican Mafia." And I was like, what? I didn't know what to say—it sounded like Hitler Youth camp to me. To prove his mafia-ness, he opened his backpack and showed me a loaded gun. This was sixth grade; we were twelve years old. So that was Raymond. His crew was pretty benign. They didn't really cause trouble, but I was keenly aware of them.

The third gang are definitely the villains of this story. They were called the SOT, which stood for—it was the stupidest name—Studs of Tafolla. To me, they were posers, a bunch of middle-class kids who got bused to our school and pretended they were in a gang. They wanted to be tough, and you had to worry about them because there were so many. They were so keen to pick fights that they were always causing trouble. I hated their guts.

The fourth, not-real gang was me and my buddies. We were the punk rock, alternative, grunge, flannel-wearing, comic-book-reading, video-game-playing nerds. That's what we did. We didn't want to be in gang culture. All we wanted to do was play basketball and listen to grunge music from Seattle. What kept us safe from the other gangs was that the biggest kid in Tafolla was in our crew. His name was Robert, but he went by Big Mac. The reason his name was Big Mac was because he was six foot three and three hundred pounds. He'd never flunked—that was just him, out of the box, pow. Nobody messed with us because of Big Mac, and I was grateful.

We were in eighth-grade gym class one day making fun of gang culture when somebody said, "Hey, we should give ourselves a name."

Someone else said, "Yeah, we can call ourselves the Cool Flannel Club."

We all started laughing, and then Big Mac said, "No, change the C to a K and we'll be KFC."

We were like, yes! And we called ourselves KFC. An unintended consequence was that as soon as we gave ourselves a name, the other gangs were like, oh, you're a gang. Then things got serious. The SOT wanted to start a fight with us. They wanted to test our gang-ness, which was the last thing we wanted.

This is what happened. One day we were playing basketball. We were in the middle of a shot, and this Doritos bag full of sand came crashing down on us. We looked, and the SOTs were there loading up another one, ready to fire. At Tafolla, kids graffitied the walls so often that the school hired a company to sandblast the walls, and there were always mounds of sand around. The SOTs had filled old Coke bottles and chip bags with sand to throw at us. They were trying to get us to start a fight so they could beat us up. We were the punk artists, though, and we didn't want to fight them.

We avoided this for weeks, until finally someone said something and these ten guys came up and faced us down. The only reason it didn't go down that day was Big Mac's six foot three inches and three hundred pounds. I was so terrified that I decided to use my street hustle. I was going to run a hustle on these guys and put an end to them.

The next day, as I was walking to lunch, I ran into Raymond, and he goes, "Hey, Lorenzo, what's up?"

And I said, "Hey. Don't you think the Studs of Tafolla are a bunch of jerks?"

He was like, "Yeah, dude, I hate those guys."

"What if we all jumped them?"

"Yeah, man, I'd be down with that."

I had just made the first chess move of my street hustle. Like Don Corleone, I said, "It's time to declare war." I was fourteen years old, by the way.

If I can just get NDs on board, I thought, *we will destroy these dudes*. I decided to make a visit to the one guy in the

NDs who loved me, Adrian. I was going to roll out my PowerPoint and walk him through my pitch on why we should jump the SOTs.

One of the horrible, violent rituals of Tafolla at that time was this thing called *carrilla*. If anybody found out it was your birthday, you got jumped. For no reason, ten guys would beat you up and throw you in the shower.

I was standing there waiting for Adrian so I could pitch him my street hustle. All of a sudden, I heard a huge commotion. Somebody said, "Hey, it's Adrian's birthday." Twenty SOTs ran into the bathroom to jump him. Then about nine NDs ran behind them to give their boy some support.

I started walking toward the bathroom to see what was happening. Then something occurred that I hadn't anticipated in my street hustle: the adults intervened. Suddenly there were fifty cops and thirty adults everywhere. I later learned that the school police officer had started a sting operation to crack down on us eighth-grade gang dudes. The day they launched the program happened to be the day Adrian's birthday went down, so they came in and arrested everybody in the fight—which didn't include me. There were two police vans full of cuffed eighth-graders, and they all got expelled. Adrian, the SOTs, and all of the NDs were gone, just like that. Me and the rest of the KFC crew got to live out the rest of eighth grade without being afraid of getting jumped.

I'm very grateful that the adults intervened, and that I'm not here telling you how I successfully orchestrated sixty fourteen-year-olds beating up another thirty fourteen-year-olds.

Cheers to the hustles we don't pull off.

Everything Was Fine
until the Violent Revolution

MIKE KNOOP

When I tell people I moved around a lot as a kid, they automatically assume that my parents were military. I think it was more a case of wanderlust. In 1975 I was a second-grader in Meadows Elementary in San Diego, California. That fall I was a third-grader at Tehran American School, the capital of Iran, or I-ran, as we say in Texas. My dad was an accountant, and he got a job with Bell Helicopter International, so we left the land of beaches and Burger King for—well, we weren't really sure. My parents had immigrated from Germany in 1968, when I was less than a year old, and they had rudimentary English skills then. But they became pretty fluent, so moving to another country where they didn't speak the language didn't seem like much of a leap.

It's worth mentioning how hard it was to access information in 1975. There was no internet, no CNN, so it was difficult to find out about a country on the other side of the world. Our main source of information was a book that Bell Helicopter's public relations team put out, *Life in Iran.* The history section didn't mention the 1951 power struggle between the Shah, Mohammad Reza Pahlavi, and his prime minister, Mohammad Mosaddegh, who was trying to nationalize the war reserves. It didn't talk about the Shah fleeing Iran, and it certainly didn't mention the 1953 coup, engineered in part by the CIA, that brought the Shah back to the throne. Instead the book focused on the Shah's White Revolution, a series of reforms meant to modernize the country, and included women's suffrage and universal compulsory education. The revolution was in full flower when we arrived in Iran in 1975.

I really feel like the Iranians thought we were awesome visitors to their country. My sister and I both had fair skin and blond, blond hair, so we were very exotic and cute as buttons at the same time. My sister quickly learned to avoid elderly Iranian women because they would pinch her cheeks and say *"krosh killeh, krosh killeh,"* which means "pretty one, pretty one."

About a year after we transferred, we tested and were accepted into the more rigorous and prestigious K–12 International Community School, with students from around the world. Along with the school change came a change of address. We moved from a house in the northern part of the city to an apartment in the heart of downtown, about two blocks from the main avenue. Every morning an Iranian driver picked us up in a blue school bus and, along with twenty or twenty-five other students and teachers, we made the thirty-minute commute to school. My dad had a driver who took him to and from work, but other than that we pretty much walked everywhere, took public transportation and the occasional taxi—typical big city living.

For a couple of years, life in Iran was great. It's hard to stress how safe it was. I was allowed to ride my bike all around downtown, and I usually headed to the super-market or a bookstore, looking for the latest issue of *Mad* magazine. One bookstore had a room overflowing with Marvel and DC comics, and since I wasn't allowed to read them at home I spent my afternoons reading them there. Really, the big drama of my life was that my dad wouldn't take me to see a movie called *Star Wars* because the the-aters were only showing it in Farsi, and I'd be like, "Dad, I don't need to understand what they're saying. I just want to see what they look like." But apart from small tragedies like that, Iran was definitely home.

Things began to change in fall 1978. I was starting sixth grade in a different part of the school, and I wasn't doing well. I had bad grades, and I was a bit of a discipline prob-lem. Turns out the country was doing even worse. The Muslim clerics were rebelling against the Shah's reform, and the Shah cracked down with martial law. SAVAK, the secret police, were suddenly part of our vocabulary. Firebombs and blackouts were pretty common. We could often hear protesters marching down the main avenue, since we lived so close, shouting "Khomeini, Khomeini"—meaning the Ayatollah Khomeini, the exiled Islamic fundamentalist cleric and leader of the revolution.

For a while life went on more or less as usual. The bus driver still picked us up, still took us home. But with the passing weeks, fewer and fewer students showed up to class. One dark November night, an incident occurred that made it impossible for my sister and me to return to class.

I don't know what sparked this riot, but it was absolutely huge. There were more protesters than we'd ever seen before. There was an angry, hostile energy in the crowd. It got dark early in November, and pretty soon it was full-on night as the bus driver slowly tried to work his way through the crowd. We saw more and more banners with ugly caricatures of Uncle Sam and President Jimmy Carter, and we saw a bunch of protesters setting American flags on fire. About this time, the bus driver had it. He turned around and said, "Get down, get down." He was talking to the three blond kids on the bus—my sister, me, and another American girl my age named Althea. We all lay down on the floor, and the other students and teachers covered us with their coats and jackets to conceal us. The crowd was pushing the bus from side to side, and we could feel it swaying. The whole time they were banging on it to make noise and shouting "Khomeini, Khomeini."

Finally, inch by inch, the bus driver made it to Althea's apartment, which was closer to the school than ours. By now his nerves were shot. He asked us to get off at Althea's stop, so my sister and I did, and her parents called our parents, and my dad picked us up with his driver.

I remember the rest of the night as uneventful, but as far as my parents were concerned that was pretty much it for Iran. Not too long after that, in March 1979, we moved to the relative safety of Fort Worth, Texas. I was kind of a gawky, gangly preteen. My only real goal was to fit in, to assimilate with American culture again, which for me could be summed up in one sentence: Don't talk about Iran.

This is honestly the most I've talked about it outside of family in almost forty years, so thank you.

Sharing Tea with Syrian Intelligence

DAVID W. LESCH

There I was in a small nondescript room at the Damascus International Airport, located just outside of Damascus, Syria. I was sitting in front of a coffee table, in a seat that was very low to the ground. Around me were Syrian intelligence officers, and across from me was a Syrian colonel, an intelligence officer, who was obviously in charge. He put a gun on the table in front of me and started spinning it around, like a game of Russian roulette. *Now I know why this room doesn't have any windows*, I thought.

How did I get there? And more importantly, how did I get out?

I'm a professor of Middle East history, and one of my specialties is Syria. I've been traveling to Syria regularly since the late 1980s, and I've developed a rather extensive network of contacts. Being an academic, obviously, a number of these contacts are in academia. When Bashar al-Assad came to power in 2000 following his father's death, he brought a number of academics into the government. Usually that's a sign of the apocalypse, but in this case it was a positive sign because it was a nontraditional class that he brought into power. One of my best friends in Syria became a cabinet minister and, to make a long story short, through him I was connected with Bashar al-Assad. I met with Assad on a regular basis in 2004 and 2005. I became something of an unofficial liaison between the U.S. government and the Syrian government, because U.S.–Syrian relations were much less than cordial at the time. In fact, if you recall, in early 2000 the George W. Bush administration listed the axis of evil as Iran, Iraq, and North Korea. Syria was, in essence, on the axis of evil's junior varsity list.

For my meetings with Assad I was typically dropped off on the Damascus airport tarmac, and two Mercedes with a security detail would whisk me to an ornate VIP room. My handlers got my bags, took care of customs, and escorted me to a nice hotel. It was all really cool. I enjoyed that part of it. Every now and then, because a president or prime minister was visiting, the office of protocol was swamped and I had to go through customs and take a taxi to the hotel. No big deal, right?

Well, in November 2007 this is what happened: I landed. No security detail, no Mercedes. *Okay*, I thought to myself. I was pretty bummed out that I wasn't getting the royal treatment. I went over to the customs officer. I wasn't worried—that is, not until the officer said, "I'm confiscating your passport." When I asked why, he showed me a piece of paper. "You're on the blacklist." Believe me, you do not want to be on the blacklist in a country like Syria. You are at the very least persona non grata, and usually much worse.

Some of the officers from Air Force Intelligence—the most powerful intelligence agency in Syria, and they control the airport—brought me into a secluded room and started asking questions. The colonel kept saying, "Why are you here? What is your mission?" And I kept saying, "I have an appointment tomorrow morning with your president. Don't you know that? You're intelligence, right? It's not a contradiction in terms. You should know that."

This went on for three hours. I think he was hoping to wear me down. He kept twirling his gun, hoping to intimidate me. It worked a little bit, but I've been through stuff like this before. If you travel to the Middle East enough, especially under circumstances like mine, guns will be pointed at you and you usually get interrogated by somebody. I wasn't freaked out—a little concerned but not freaked out. It wasn't the end of the world.

Into the third hour I finally convinced the colonel that it was in his best interest to call the president's office and confirm that I had an appointment. I told him he would be in worse trouble if he didn't. He finally gave in and called. It was almost worth the ordeal to see his mouth open wide, his face go pale. He got off the phone, and all of a sudden, he was apologetic. "Wow," he said, "the office told me that you meet the president often; they told me that you wrote a book about him."

Then he said, "Can I have your autograph?" And irony of ironies, he couldn't find a sheet of paper, so he took out the blacklist with my name on it and turned it over, and I signed that. We had some tea and talked about our families. He escorted me from the airport, and I was driven to the hotel. Everything was cool.

The next morning, I met with Assad. As he usually does, he asked how my trip was. I said other than the confiscation of my passport, the blacklist, and the three-hour interrogation, it was fine. He was aghast. He said, "I'm going to send somebody to find out more about this."

This was a case of the left hand of intelligence not knowing what the right hand of government was doing. I was known in Syria. It was known that I was meeting with the president, yet intelligence didn't know about it, or chose not to know about it. Syrian intelligence, or what is called the Mukhabarat, have a lot of leeway, and Assad, knowing he is in a dangerous neighborhood, gives them this leeway. Finally, I told him—we had the type of rapport at the time where I could be fairly frank—"Mr. President, if you don't get control of these guys, they're going to come back and haunt you."

Sure enough, these were somewhat prophetic words. In March 2011 the Mukhabarat arrested, roughed up, and tortured some teenagers who had painted antiregime graffiti on a wall in Daraa, a small town in southern Syria. Their hubris was the match that lit the flame to an uprising and then civil war.

When I left Assad that day, he said it would never happen again. Three months later, in February 2008, it happened again when I arrived. Confiscated and brought to the room, except it was the same colonel, who obviously hadn't lost his job. He hugged me and said it was all right. We had tea again, and he escorted me to the hotel.

And you know, this is a problem in Syria. I've been there a number of times since then, even a couple of times during the civil war, where on one occasion we had a rather harrowing visit to Damascus. I hope to go back sometime soon, when it's safe, and when this horrific chapter in Syria is only in the history books—and when I don't appear on the blacklist anymore.

Grateful

REY LOPEZ

It's August 2015, and I'm standing in an empty apartment in downtown San Antonio with nothing but the clothes in my suitcase. I have no furniture. I have no food. I don't even have anyone to talk to. And that's when it hits me: I've always shared my living space with somebody, even as an only child, whether it was my parents, or wife and kids, or roommates. For the first time, at the age of fifty, I'm living alone.

Well, now what? I ask myself. The answer to that question will take me on a journey I never expected while all the institutions I have given my life to fall apart around me.

You see, I never feel like I quite fit in. I can be in a room full of friendly faces, but I always feel like I'm missing something everybody else seems to get. Maybe that's what led me to become part of an evangelical Christian community as a college student. For more years than I was married, I gave everything I was to that community. I went on mission trips. I volunteered with my church. I even left my job at USAA to go back to school. I went to seminary and got ordained, and I served huge congregations, even a big multisite megachurch in San Antonio. But for all those decades that I served as a pastor, I still never felt like I quite fit in.

If you know anything about evangelical Christians, you know they believe that they have the corner on truth, that their understanding of Christianity is absolutely correct, to the exclusion of not only every other Christian denomination but every other religion. That they think they have the corner on truth never sat well with me, but I never felt comfortable bringing up questions.

When I was going through my divorce and had all these questions I couldn't bring up, there were two defining moments in my life. The first was a book I read, *Scary Close*, by Donald Miller. Miller talks about his struggle to maintain relationships and how he had to learn to take off his mask and live authentically. The second was a podcast by the Liturgists—but don't be fooled by the name. They are a decidedly irreligious group of people who are having conversations and making safe spaces to express doubt. The podcast featured the kinds of conversations I didn't think anyone was having, certainly not within the evangelical community. The first episode I listened to was "Black and White America," and as I listened to the hosts talk about racism both subtle and not so subtle, I began to realize I was an unwitting participant in a community—in a system—of belief that marginalized not only people of color but whole groups of people. The best way I can describe what was happening to me as I listened was like when you're watching *The Wizard of Oz* and it goes from black-and-white to color. I began to understand that the binary this-or-that way of thinking is not how the world works.

I was going through all these transitions in my thinking, from racism to politics to sexuality and every other issue you can imagine, and I'm doing a complete 180 from the way I used to think. Right around this time, the last church I worked at was going through an upheaval. They said it was a reorganization, but it was an upheaval. And it was brutal. They gave me two options: I could stay and take a 25 percent pay cut, or I could walk away with three months' severance. At first, in my desire to fit in, I decided I would stay, even though I would effectively be making less money than I had twenty years earlier, fresh out of seminary. It was like staying in a toxic relationship because you think being alone is worse. Then I remembered something Donald Miller wrote in *Scary Close*, about how the greatest regret of the dying is that they didn't live lives that were true to themselves, and instead lived lives other people expected them to. That's when I knew I needed to walk away. And I did. I did.

I started to dismantle all these old ways of thinking. Then there was another watershed event, the presidential election of 2016. I watched in disbelief as all these people I had spent decades working with, and doing life with, so easily compromised the values they said they clung to so that they could have their guy in power. That was the last straw.

In the years that followed—and I continue to shift my ways of thinking—I've been able to create a community of people who have gone through the same things I have. I'm back at USAA, and I'm in a relationship with a woman who shows me every day what it means to love. As I tell this story, it occurs to me that when I walked into my apartment in August 2015, it was thirty years to the month that I had waded into the waters of Evangelicalism. It was as though all the institutions I've been a part of were conspiring to blow up at the same time so I could go on this journey. And I'm grateful for that. I'm grateful I lost all those things at the same time, so I could be where I am today. And I'll tell you now, I'm looking forward to what the next thirty years reveal for me.

The Neighborhood of My Childhood

VANESSA MARTINEZ

Lots of states have a Highland Park, but the one in San Antonio is nothing like the wealthy suburb in Dallas or the city in Illinois. San Antonio's Highland Park is a neighborhood near downtown where working-class citizens have lived since the early 1900s. Bedrooms in these homes have separate exit doors so families could rent out rooms that weren't needed. Or maybe they were needed, but the rent money was needed more. No million-dollar mansions exist in this Highland Park, but it was my neighborhood.

By the time I was old enough to observe things, I noticed the older people leaving. The original German and white families moved away, and their children sold the homes to families like mine: Mexican Americans trying to give their children middle-class lives. White flight, I learned later. The neighborhood wasn't fancy, but I loved it.

My sister and I could do whatever we wanted on those streets. They were ours. We went to the convenience store next door to buy our favorites—minipies, cupcakes, and other cheap sweets. We picked pecans for pennies and took the money to Star Pharmacy, where we bought gum for three cents or Chinese candies for a nickel or a dime. We never really wanted for anything outside of our neighborhood. Everything we needed was within walking or driving distance. We had mom-and-pop shops. We had laundromats. We had restaurants. We had a big grocery store. We had a bakery called Mr. and Mrs. Johnson's, and the couple who owned it made the best donuts and cinnamon rolls. I've never found any quite as good since they retired and closed. I walked to school safely, and in high school I used the city bus system to and from campus. That house and those shops, those streets, they were home.

We had this amazing neighbor, Mr. Vela, who made us and others feel like we were part of the community all the time. He loved to offer us candies, chips, popcorn balls, popcorn balls, and popcorn balls. He always had a popcorn ball on him—almost always Halloween-packaged ones, even after Halloween was long over. A few years into my adulthood I realized that Mr. Vela was probably a hoarder and had a closet of popcorn balls. But the fact that he thought of us made my sister and me feel special. In an area of town with rising crime and poverty, Mr. Vela and others like him made us feel safe and connected.

Neighborhood love aside, Highland Park is also historically connected to San Antonio. I like to think of it as a little King William on the city's southeast side. All the houses are pretty much the same as the ones in the more celebrated King William. You've got Craftsman-style bungalows. You've got majestic two- and three-story buildings. There are even Japanese Craftsman bungalows. The neighborhood, when lawns were kept and houses were tidy, was small but beautiful.

Besides the emotional, historical, and community spirit, my street—and my home, in fact—have a cool little story. In 1977 my house was picked for a movie. If you've never heard of the film *Rolling Thunder*, don't worry. I hadn't heard of it until one day when my mom mentioned that in 1979, when she and my father bought the home, someone from the movie tried to steal the French doors (which I thought were creepy and old) during the real estate transfer.

Rolling Thunder, which Gene Siskel considered one of the top ten films of 1977, stars William Devane and Tommy Lee Jones. Quentin Tarantino thought enough of it to call his first production company Rolling Thunder Productions.

I hadn't thought about the movie in years, but one day I decided to look it up. I found the film broken into eight parts on YouTube, so I was able to watch the whole thing. For free. It's a really good movie. If you have enough time to watch eight parts of something on YouTube, you should look it up. It's the story of a Vietnam vet who loses his family—and his right arm—during a home invasion, and in true Tarantino fashion, gruesome revenge ensues. If you go nine minutes into the seventh YouTube clip, you'll see my childhood home. William Devane is visiting Tommy Lee Jones, supposedly in El Paso, but he's actually in San Antonio, in Highland Park, in my living room.

I tried to listen to the dialogue, but it's kind of hard to pay attention when you're imagining yourself in the exact same place they are. I saw our beautiful mailbox that's built into the custom windows at the front of our house—which wasn't practically thought out and led to mail spilling everywhere when it dropped through the slot four feet from the floor. I saw our beautiful hand-carved wooden mantle. I saw our bookshelves with our baby pictures and trophies, warmly lit in yellow, quiet and still after we all went to bed.

Back to the revenge: Bill and Tommy decide to get down to business and talk, so they leave the living room and go to my bedroom. They pull a bag of guns from the same closet that will hold my quinceañera dresses in the future. The closet of my Keds, my loafers. They take the guns, run out through my bedroom's French doors (that someone tried to steal) and down our red granite steps, and walk over to Mr. Vela's driveway—which really bothers my mom, because "we have a great driveway they could've used!" They drive down the street.

I saw my street, in my Highland Park, at night. I saw the beautiful trees. I saw the lights. I saw the buildings, and I wish I could tell you the street was the same, but it's not. When the older people left or passed, when their children sold their homes to move to the suburbs, my community, like many, lost the connections that had been created by the generations before. Some decided to rent the homes their parents had left them and let them get run-down. Those of us who moved in and were trying to build middle-class lives didn't have access to wealth to keep things up, but we did the best we could. Shops closed. We persisted, and we lived, and as the homes became cheaper we created different communities that supported each other in different ways. More *molinos*, more *panaderías*. More people like me, making moves to build some semblance of wealth.

Now that the community is full of people who want to make more, to be more, things are changing again. White flight has turned into white boomerang. Homes that were disregarded are important again as suburbs fill with diverse communities that have bought into the promise of prosperity. Downtown is cool again, and so is the property. Families like mine are being pushed out again as our neighborhood becomes unaffordable to those who helped it survive for four decades.

As I watch the back and forth, I think of the things I want. I want my Highland Park back. I want community, security, and spirit. I want the beautiful homes where people thrived, and I want diversity and respect. I want people to fight for my neighborhood like my parents fought for those French doors, like Tommy Lee Jones and William Devane fought to avenge family and limbs. I want my grandbabies to walk down the red granite steps that Tommy Lee Jones walked down, knowing that those steps are important, just like they are.

How I Became a Brony

COLLIN McGRATH

I'd had dreams of being the lead in a school musical since elementary school. My voice changed, so it didn't happen in eighth grade. I got roles in every high school play, even Ebenezer Scrooge my senior year, but never that singing role I wanted. On one hand, I wasn't talented enough. I had singing flaws that wouldn't be corrected until I worked with a college music professor. And I only ever acted for fun. I definitely had some stiffness in my posture. On the other hand, our director had a peculiar habit. He gave the biggest singing roles to the students he knew could win awards and bring the school acclaim. My junior and senior years, he recruited transfer students and cast junior students for the lead roles. All my loyalty and dedication apparently meant nothing to him. It hurt, given that I once saw this director as a second father.

High school theater was the second time in my life where I felt so hurt by a man I wanted to love. The first time I can remember is my dad waking me for school. He was yelling, "Wake up, slowpoke. How many times I got to tell you?"

He yelled at me a lot, but he could be patient too. I doubt many dads could watch *Star Wars: Revenge of the Sith* and the second *X-Man* movie a dozen nights in a row. Few dads would bring their kids to the office and let them play the *Land Before Time* game on their work computer. Of course, most dads don't verbally abuse their sons. Sometimes I still think he's on an extended business trip and not dead from an alcohol-ruptured pancreas.

High school was a time of theater, but it was also a time for watching cartoons with my little sister. I already knew one of them through a sort of cultural osmosis via YouTube videos. The name of the show? *My Little Pony: Friendship Is Magic.* The show focuses on the life of unicorn Twilight Sparkle, her five pony friends, and one baby dragon learning how friendship is, well, magic. It has a unique fandom called the Bronies.

What is a Brony, you ask? A Brony is a male or adult who enjoys the *My Little Pony: Friendship Is Magic* series or the fan community. And, yes, it is contagious. I should know. When we ran out of stuff to watch one night, my sister said, "Hey, do you want to watch some *My Little Pony*?"

"Go for it," I said. I handed her the remote and started playing Pokémon on my DS. The first episode we watched together was about Flutter Shy learning to overcome her stage fright. I wasn't particularly impressed. I watched the show on my own sometimes, but I never actively sought it out until I watched a marathon of episodes about a dragon named Spike.

Twilight Sparkle hatches Spike from an egg as part of her magical entrance exam and adopts him. He becomes her number one assistant, penning and delivering letters to Princess Celestia. My toy drawer is stuffed with intricate dragon figures. As a child, I believed they existed like I believed in God. So, Spike the dragon caught my attention.

Compared to the others, his character seemed to have infinitely more potential. I kept waiting for the show to explore his relationship with Twilight, the fact that he never knew his parents, or how he felt about being the only dragon in a town of ponies. Yet he never really got the spotlight. It certainly bugged me, but those thoughts were in the back of my mind when I graduated from high school and headed to college.

Theater didn't turn out well for me. I gave it my all, but even when I really got into a scene and felt like I had it down, people would say I looked unnatural. It's a huge blow to your confidence when your talent at the thing you've enjoyed for the last four years is called into question. Another freshman seemed to have theater success without really trying, which made me feel even more inadequate. I seemed to butt heads with some of the other students when I didn't mean any offense. So many times I just wanted to go to sleep and never wake up again. I considered acting on that impulse. If I couldn't succeed at the one thing I knew I was good at, the thing that defined me in high school, what was the point? I felt so alone. It was as though my entire existence was being threatened.

My therapist and family talked me out of that dark line of thought, but the rest of the year was unhappy, save for the nights I watched *My Little Pony* videos on YouTube. The animations and music videos were just a lot of fun—although they further fueled my daydreams of an episode that utilized Spike's potential. By the time Christmas break rolled around, I had imagined half a dozen Spike stories. Since I couldn't speak to the show writers and tell them my brilliant ideas, they were doomed to stay in my head. Finally, a thought occurred to me, something so simple and yet so life-changing: *I should write those Spike stories down.*

I discovered a *My Little Pony* fanfiction site. I wrote my first story, not caring if others would read it or if it came out poorly. It was cathartic and vicarious. I truly lost myself in the process, seeing every detail unfold in my mind. And then I went a step further and published it. That first thumbs up filled me with joy. It was confirmation that at least one person enjoyed my work. I couldn't stop grinning. So, I wrote two more stories. Soon I had not just thumbs up but comments—actual comments by real human beings who liked my work.

My stories truly blew up in the spring semester. My most popular story took inspiration from the *Star Trek: The Next Generation* episode "The Measure of a Man." In my telling, Twilight leads a defense trial to prove that Spike is entitled to the same rights as any pony and cannot be used as a lab rat to study dragons. Within days of publishing the first two chapters, the story went viral, getting more attention than anything I'd written before. And believe me, I loved every second of the popularity— hundreds of upvotes and comments, people emailing me with fan art of my story's original characters and saying the story helped them through personal issues. All this, from a story I wrote for fun.

After four years of college, I ended my fanfiction career with seventeen stories totaling more than half a million words and a scholarship to Simmons College, where I received master's and master of fine arts degrees in children's literature. Now I'm drafting my own stories with the hopes of one day being published. But I never quite forgot everything that writing, *My Little Pony* fandom, and Spike gave me. *My Little Pony* helped me overcome my depression and self-loathing after countless theatrical failures. And Spike was the character who spurred my new life dedicated to writing. He was the dragon who made me a Brony.

Live, Laugh, Lowride

JOAQUIN MUERTE

My name is Joaquin. Everybody knows me as Joaquin Muerte, but my government name is Joaquin Abrego. I come from Del Rio, a typical small Texas town on the border. I'm from the San Felipe barrio. I come from two cholo parents—my mom, old-school chola, they called her "the teenager," and my dad, Raúl, un pachuco, they called him "lowrider." They were both very hard-core, involved in gangs, but when their gang member friends started to die from gun violence, they decided to organize their community. They were introduced to the Brown Berets and started as social justice activists organizing around immigrant rights—organizing of all kinds, turning gang members into teammates and building lowriders out of cars and just random bike parts to lowrider bikes. As a part of that they began doing work for *Lowrider* magazine, and they went from there. I was born in 1982, nine months after a crazy LSD trip/love fest to the tune of "You Can't Hide Love" by Earth, Wind & Fire.

I jumped right into social justice activism. I was a little boy folding chairs, wiping down tables, and helping out people in the community as much as I could. I joined every little project my mom was a part of. But both my parents were super busy, always out in the community. One of the things we fought about all the time was food. We ate really bad and drank a lot of alcohol. I started drinking as a young kid, and when I say young, I was about fifteen. Life on the border and access to Mexico was easy. It was always like, warm up some nuggets. Get a little microwavable pizza. Make a sandwich. *Sangwich.* You put the chips on the inside and crunch it closed.

The barrio where I grew up was very much like the West Side of San Antonio, but the barrio has a beautiful river on the inside that flows right through. We were always in the water. Swimming was a big thing in our hood. As my parents were organizing in the park, doing stuff with gangs, driving lowriders, and painting murals, we would swim.

Fast-forward. When I wanted to go to college and moved to San Antonio, back around 2000, I was still struggling with my relationship with food. I was always eating the same nuggets and making the same sandwich. Quick microwavable pizzas. Yum! I got involved with the Chicano movement and put my skill set to use, meeting local social justice organizations and on-the-ground Chicano efforts. I got connected with places like the Esperanza Peace and Justice Center. The people there knew me and would say, "Mijo, how are your parents? Come in, we need your help," and I would jump right into it. I was organizing with places like Fuerza Unida. They'd say, "¿Cómo estás, mijo? ¿Cómo están tu mamá y tu papá?" They knew me as a kid, but I was an adult now, learning how to organize with them, learning the San Antonio landscape of organizing. All the while eating like shit.

I started to get involved with some crust punks because, you know, Chicanos are also crust punks. In that circle there was a lot of veganism and vegetarianism; we're protesting meat companies, and we're eating vegetables. So, for me, how do you find vegetarian nuggets, right? There wasn't the healthy alternative stuff we see now. It was hard to undo that comfort. I was eating a lot of bread and pasta, and I was just putting on the weight. This has always been a big battle for me.

In the circle of DIY crust and punk rockers, I began doing a lot of protest work. Organizing massive protests in San Antonio was my new skill set. I started working for the Southwest Workers Union, and one year we were protesting the treatment of immigrants in San Antonio. We were arm-locked, making a human chain outside city hall, and I saw my homeboy Juan cruising by on his ten-speed mountain bike—that dude went everywhere by bike. "Hey, Joaquin," he yelled, "what the fuck are you doing?"

"You know, holding it down, man!" I yelled back.

We had all the intersections in front of city hall blocked, there were cops all over the place, and we were chanting the whole time. And he said, "Hey, man, the city is looking for community organizers like you."

My thought was, *Work for the man? Hell, naw!* But literally that year, the organization started to push out some of our old-school organizers, and I decided to leave. I got a job with the city. They were looking for a community health worker, someone who organized around health and equity. Me and health? Well, I'm an organizer, I'll figure it out. I wanted to community organize, to continue that work and keep working for the people on the ground, my people. And I figured, well, if I like to eat chicken nuggets, how can I do it healthy, right? I jumped right into it. They wanted me to do food demos, show people how to drink more water and eat healthier in the San Anto barrios. *Órale*, I got this.

We made aguas frescas without sugar by mixing cucumber lemon or watermelon mint. It was infused water. Aguas frescas literally translates to fresh waters. Everybody loved it. I started to bang *pesado* (work hard) on the city's West Side, going to every organization, everybody I knew, everybody I was working with on the ground, offering this new knowledge. I made healthy versions of enchiladas verdes, caldo de pollo, even vegan caldo, substituting the pollo with mushrooms. I showed people how to make healthy carne guisada by substituting flour gravy with cornstarch gravy. It was crazy how much I was getting around.

Then Covid hit, and we were all told to do Covid response. Then snowmageddon, and now we were doing mutual aid. Snowmageddon in Del Rio created a freak snow. It snowed twelve inches, and my parents were snowed in their home. They ran out of food and water, and they were already not eating well. At one point my mom said all they had was tequila. Dead serious! They were surviving in the freezing temperatures like that big cartoon Saint Bernard dog all drunk with the barrel of liquor around its neck.

After the snow cleared my father started acting weird, so we decided to take him to the hospital. Turns out he'd had a series of strokes. He was hospitalized, and soon after he moved in with me. The doctors said, "You want to save him? You have to help him eat healthy." I cooked for him every day, making the same recipes I used in the communities I was organizing. I talked the talk, and now it was time to walk the walk.

He would say stuff like, "¡Qué es esto! ¿Comida de conejo?"

And I was like, "Yeah, man, it's healthy. You have to try it."

"Well, I want something for breakfast. Give me some bacon and eggs."

I made him turkey bacon with kale and eggs. Mixed it all together with a little bit of mushroom, and he loved it. In protest, he would say, "What is this?" Then he would taste it, and I would ask him if he liked it, and he'd be like, "It's pretty good."

I was taking pictures of every meal and posting them on social media and talking about the process, including things like sobriety. My father had to be sober. He couldn't drink the way he used to, couldn't smoke cigarettes. I decided to give up drinking alcohol with him. I started exercising and eating the recipes—because I was making enough for all of us, including my mom. I kept posting all of this and titled the food blog "How to Tame the Southern Texas Border Brown Man."

I got a call from a friend of mine, Keli Cabunoc. An agency working with the Food Network had contacted her looking for local chefs, and she told them, "Forget local chefs, I know some really good cooks in the neighborhood to feature."

She said, "Hey, the Food Network's looking for somebody." And I was like, "Hell, yeah! I'm down." A month later the Food Network called and said, "Hey, we're ready for you." And I was like, "Oh shit, she was serious?" They asked me to put a recipe on paper and practice it so I could be prepared to film it. They loved my recipe, but I couldn't *tantear* the spices—they wanted to know specifics. I told them I spiced until my dead ancestor yelled, "¡Ya, mijo, that's enough!"

I was featured on the Food Network, y'all. Look me up. It was amazing. Within hours thousands of people had liked the video. My father's health improved. Using the knowledge that I shared with the community, I was able to get my father's health in order.

Punk Rock, Leather Bars, and Life on the Road

SANFORD NOWLIN

Most rock 'n' roll tours are more about excruciatingly long drives and sleep deprivation than they are about drugged debauchery. Most touring rock musicians spend twenty hours out of the day living like truck drivers so we can spend that one hour each night coming alive on stage. Of course, if there's a little time left over for some budget bacchanalia, we're okay with that, too.

My story of life on the road begins with me and my band at the time, Boxcar Satan, during a 2005 tour. We were nearly a month in, it was seven in the morning, and we were waking up on the living room floor of my friend Derek in Seattle. We'd slept three hours, and we all stunk of beer from the night before. Derek started making coffee and turned on the TV. The newscaster was warning that Seattle rush hour would be especially brutal. Some of the worst fog in ages had rolled into town, turning the highways into parking lots.

As my drummer, Ken, rolled up his sleeping bag, he said, "Hey, uh, how many hours did you say it was to our gig in San Francisco?"

"Thirteen," I said, wincing.

Next thing you know we were in the van, plunging into the dense Seattle fog. It felt like cruising through the set of a Hammer horror film. My bass player, Patrick, despite a third-degree hangover, had volunteered to take first shift.

Even though Boxcar Satan had a cult following around the country, we couldn't afford perks like a tour bus, a driver, or a road manager. We were known for tempering our postpunk aggression with blues, free jazz, eastern European folk music, and even gospel. And while all that eclecticism and sonic wanderlust is fun for a musician, it doesn't make for tunes that get you played on MTV or stocked on the shelves at Walmart.

There's a long history of groups who came before us and inspired this scattergun approach. One was a band in the early 1980s from Texas called the Dicks. The Dicks created an especially volatile mashup of blues and punk, fronted by this raspy-voiced guy named Gary Floyd who wore his left-wing politics and sexuality on his shirtsleeve. He often performed in drag. I can only imagine how that went over in 1981—performing in front of a bunch of Texas good old boys while dressed like Divine and singing songs full of Marxist politics. I'm sure it pissed off a lot of people.

But that kind of tenacity, that willingness to offend, was inspiring to Boxcar Satan. Even though we could depend on record store employees and other musical weirdos to come to our shows, and rock critics generally gave us positive reviews, most of the rest of the country couldn't figure out what the hell we were trying to do.

Back to the road story. By the time we cleared Seattle, about two and a half hours later, the fog had turned into rain. The I-5 was slick, and traffic was slowing down again. It looked unlikely we would make the San Francisco gig on time. We didn't eat breakfast, we didn't eat lunch—and we pissed in Gatorade bottles so we wouldn't have to stop for bathroom breaks.

By the time we hit the California line, things were getting worse. The check engine light flashed on. We knew if we pulled off to get it checked out, we'd probably miss the gig. At the same time, we didn't want to burn up our engine. We found a gas station near Redding, only to learn that the mechanic had already left for the day.

The guy behind the register looked us up and down, taking in our disheveled and desperate appearance, and said, "Are you dudes in a band?"

When we admitted the obvious, he told us he had played in punk groups when he was younger but never got the chance to release any records or tour. After he learned we were from Texas, he praised the intensity of the state's litany of strange underground bands. "Oh, man, you guys had the Butthole Surfers, you had Scratch Acid, you had the Big Boys, you had the Dicks."

At least for that moment, the guy was living vicariously through us. Something about these three beer-stinking morons wandering into his gas station had rekindled his memories of playing music, his long-abandoned aspirations to gig on the road. It made me realize we couldn't blow up our San Francisco gig on account of some measly check engine light. How many times had that stupid thing come on over something minor like, I don't know, a faulty air sensor?

The guy at the gas station would kill to be in our shoes. Screw the light. We needed to forge ahead.

We armed ourselves with stale sandwiches and more Gatorade bottles to piss in and headed into San Francisco. We were only an hour late for load-in time, and the engine didn't burn out.

But there was a new twist. We realized the venue we'd been booked at, the Eagle Tavern, was a leather bar in the Castro. The sparse crowd was a bunch of middle-aged gentlemen with handlebar mustaches and leather chaps. It wasn't our normal crowd, let's just say.

We started to worry. Were we in the right place? If we played, would we get paid? Next thing you know, Patrick peeled a flier off the wall and held it up to me. My jaw dropped. We were opening for Gary Floyd and his band at the time, the Bad Ride. Yeah, the raspy-voiced guy from the Dicks.

Turns out Thursday was punk rock night at the Eagle, and we were playing Gary Floyd's fiftieth birthday party. Talk about kismet. We started setting up on stage, and people started filing into the club, and it was music fans of all kinds—gay, straight, transgender, you name it. And there, sitting at the end of the bar, was Gary Floyd, looking a little older but still impossible to miss.

We hit the first note of our opening song with the ferocity you'd expect from guys who just spent fifteen hours in a freaking van. And the crowd responded in kind. They came to the front of the stage, whooping and hollering, pumping their fists. The further we got into our set, the crazier it got. At one point I looked up from one of our eastern European–inspired tunes and saw two of the guys with handlebar mustaches and chaps kicking up their legs in a Russian-style dance.

When it was all over, we had the longest line at the merchandise table of our whole tour. Gary Floyd gave us a shout-out from the stage. "How about that Boxcar Satan? Those Texas boys are the real shit, don't ya think?" At the end of the night I found myself at the bar, sitting next to Gary, who was wearing one of our T-shirts. We talked about how lonely it was growing up weirdos in Texas during the 1970s and '80s. He gave me a big bear hug.

It was one of those magical gigs. And as we loaded up our van, the meaning of life on the road came into sharp focus. Touring is insanity—it's an endurance test, and it's not for everybody. You eat bad food, you drive fifteen hours with a flashing check engine light, you worry that your engine is about to drop out onto the ground. You end up in dingy green rooms with toilets that don't flush. But you do it for nights like that.

And maybe, more importantly, you're not just doing it for yourself. You're doing it for the guy at the gas station who never had the chance to go on tour but really wishes he could have. You do it for the music fan who worked long hours in a cubicle and is staying up late to pay seven bucks to see some band from Texas she's never even heard of. And you do it for legends like Gary Floyd, who went through the same endurance test and maybe doesn't have a penny to show for it, but would love to know they're passing on a legacy by inspiring someone else to do the same.

If that's not worth trucking twenty hours a day for, I don't know what is.

The Dropout Who Teaches High School

TORI POOL

About five school years ago, I got my first job in education. I was so excited and full of nerves. I remember waiting in a classroom for my peers to arrive so we could have our first level meeting. I was sitting at a tiny desk that I didn't fit in, so I was super uncomfortable. As the other teachers arrived, I could see that they had all obviously formed a relationship. They knew one another, they had inside jokes, they were laughing and talking about the summer. I was like, *great*.

The meeting started and the level leader handed out an agenda, passing around a novel along with it. When the book reached my hands, I froze. It was *To Kill a Mockingbird*, and I had never read it. As my peers started to discuss how we would teach it, I sunk into my chair and tried to be invisible. Suddenly, I missed the cue to speak. Seven pairs of eyes were on me.

I met their gaze and said, "Yes?"

They repeated the question. "Ms. Pool? Any input?"

I had a moment of panic. *Maybe I can lie*, I thought, because I had heard things about the book. I'd heard Atticus, and I'd heard Finch, and I'd heard something about a courtroom and the racist South. *I got this*, I thought. *Mockingbird* is racism in the South. But instead I decided to be honest. "Apologies," I said. "I've never read it."

The room erupted in snickers and side conversation. I sank even further in my chair. One of the teachers laughed and said, "Well, what were you doing in high school?"

Immediately, my defense mechanisms kicked in. I got annoyed and curt. "I'm sorry," I said. "I was probably getting high or skipping school, but don't worry. I understand racism."

All those snickers suddenly stopped. I was met with arched eyebrows and annoyed faces. I sank further into the chair, wishing the moment away, and said nothing for the rest of the meeting. The group didn't have any more questions for the former stoner.

I was different from those educators in that room. I'm a high school dropout who teaches high school. I'm also someone who was pulled out of middle school for a week for wearing black-cherry lipstick because my mom feared I'd join a gang. I was raised in the middle school of *Days of Our Lives* and *Another World*. Ask me anything about Jamie or Stefan and I can tell you their backstory. But I missed things like algebra, biology, and how to diagram a sentence properly. I still don't know how to diagram one. It's difficult.

I went back to school so I could be an anchor that I never had. I didn't find allies. Instead, I was met with faces in the break room who didn't want to talk to the drop-out. A lot of times it felt like *Mean Girls* but older. Way older. Instead of compliments, the comments were biting. It was, "I really like your dress, but I wouldn't have worn those shoes." Followed by, "Why are you buying book-shelves? You know these kids don't read." It was a lot of, maybe if I stayed silent and still and their vision was based on movement, they wouldn't see me.

The isolation they created, the way they made me feel like I didn't belong, forced me into the classroom. I ar-rived early. I stayed late. I ate lunch in my room, and stu-dents started to trickle in. It was magical because I started to form a bond with them that I wouldn't have had if I was gossiping in the break room. I had José come in and argue about having to read *Romeo and Juliet* out loud because, "Miss, that makes me sound gay." I convinced Teresa to let me talk to her boss about getting her a good job rec-ommendation. These were things the adults in their lives couldn't do. But I was willing to do them.

I got used to students being there before and after school. So, it didn't seem unusual when Teresa showed up one day outside my classroom. What was odd were the tears streaming down her face. I opened the door to let her in and gave her a moment to herself. I just waited. When she finally spoke, I wasn't ready for the things coming out of her mouth. She told me her stepfather had been abusing her for the past six months. She told me she confessed to her mother, and her mother didn't believe her. She told me she had been turned away from the counselor the day before when she tried to report it.

My heart broke. But my training kicked in. I said, "All right, we're going to the counselor." Teresa was scared, so I told her I would stay with her every step of the way, and I did. I was there when the police arrived, I was there for reporting, and I was there when her grandmother took her. I still think about her to this day.

Atticus Finch said this thing about being able to walk around in someone's skin, about not really knowing who they were unless you could take their perspective. I'm abbreviating because I'm a stoner, formerly. I apologize. But I understood the message. I understood these kids because I was a fuckup like them. I will advocate for them every day of my life. The most valuable advice I've ever given these kids is to rise above and to kill 'em with kindness.

And so, to those teachers who didn't believe in me that first time around, or that second time around, thank you kindly.

Forever Changed

WENDY SHELDON RIGBY

I have lived a charmed life. I grew up in San Antonio in a loving family with my father, my mother, and my older sister, Shelly. We lived a comfortable middle-class exis- tence—privileged, without much heartache, or fear, or stress. We were always taught that faith, education, and kindness are important in life. We know life isn't fair, but we also know life is beautiful.

My sister and I share many things besides the obvious genetics that make us look and sound alike. We've shared happy holidays, family vacations, joys and accomplish- ments, failures and sorrows. And as young adults, like many young women, we shared our frustrations over bad haircuts and bad boyfriends. As adults, we have the good fortune to live in the same city, both married, both mem- bers of the same church. And, as serendipity would have it, we were pregnant with our daughters at the exact same time. We shared baby showers, and we shared two beau- tiful baby girls who were born three weeks apart. The un- twin twins, the twisted sisters, we called them. Cousins, but more.

My sister is humble, brilliant, and pretty. She's pretty funny, too. She's a voracious reader. She loves live musical theater. She loves to travel. She once hiked to the bottom of the Grand Canyon and back. Her work is speech therapy in San Antonio. She has a husband and daughter who adore her. My sister is all these things. My sister is also dead.

This is not a story about cancer or an accident, or even murder. This is a story about suicide. On a scalding 103-degree day in June 2009, my sister took her own life. She killed herself in the late afternoon, and it took police several hours to pinpoint her identity, so I didn't find out until the middle of the night when I received that phone call, that phone call no one ever wants to receive. *What? No. Who has it all and throws it all away?*

The illness that made my sister do the unthinkable, the most tragic of all human decisions, is bipolar disorder. She wasn't diagnosed with this in her late teens or early twenties, like most people who have it. No, it took an unexpected job loss and the subsequent downward spiral to reveal this diagnosis at the age of fifty-one. I think my sister had been coping with it for many years, hiding it well with her smarts, and her courage, and her guts, and also perhaps with a little bit of denial. After she lost her job, when I found out about job openings I would say, "Hey, why don't you apply for this one?"

She finally told me, "Wendy, don't you understand? I will never work again."

I knew then that something was off. Like, really off. The system failed my sister, like it does so many people with serious mental illness.

When she made a suicide threat, her husband took her to the ER, which was the right thing to do. They transferred her to a psychiatric hospital, where she stayed for a week. One week, seven days, to adjust to medications and find the therapy that might help her. She was released, and two weeks later she was cleared to drive a car, the vehicle she would use to carry out her plan to kill herself.

In retrospect, my sister must have felt like she was on fire, and she would do anything, anything, to put out the flames. I never thought I would get that call at two in the morning. I never thought I would have to drive to my eighty-year-old father's house, wake him up, and tell him that his oldest child, his baby, had caused her own death. He fell to his knees and cried out to God. It was the worst moment of my life. It was the worst sorrow I had ever witnessed.

When I went out to my car that night, it started raining, and my car wouldn't start. I remember thinking to myself, in that moment, *I will never be truly happy ever again.* Suicide doesn't just happen to the person who makes that ill-fated decision to end it all; it's like a pebble thrown into the middle of a pond. The initial act makes a splash, and then the ripples grow and grow until they expand over the entire pond, everyone that person has ever known or loved.

When death is sudden, the decisions that must be made are overwhelming.

Understandably, my sister's husband could hardly speak or stand in the days following her death, much less pick out songs for a funeral or tell all the people who wanted to know what had happened. Much of that responsibility fell to me. I cannot begin to describe the empty surreal sensation of going to Stein Mart to buy burial clothes for your suddenly dead sister. I was asked to speak at her funeral. That was an act of sheer will, and to this day I'm not sure how I did it, except that I had to.

Next came self-doubt. It happened to her, could it happen to me? Am I crazy? If I start to lose it, will anybody I love know to pull me off the ledge? What about my children? What about my niece? Are they destined for devastating mental illness now or when they're fifty-one?

You see, here's the thing about suicide: no one knows how to talk about it. After my sister's death, well-meaning friends and coworkers would welcome me back, but few people said the one thing I really needed to hear: I'm sorry for your loss. If my sister had died from illness, or a car wreck, or homicide, that would have been acknowledged. But suicide is like the elephant in the room. Everyone knows it's there, everyone knows what happened, but they don't know how to talk about it, so they don't. And the stigma goes on.

Luckily, in my own family, we were able to have that conversation about suicide, and how to prevent it, and it's a conversation we continue to have. Celebrations without my sister are still so hard. Birthdays, holidays, high school graduations, college graduations, my son's wedding. My niece has a great dad. A great dad who has given her love and counseling to come out of this thing with grace and confidence. But every fifteen-year-old girl needs her mother. When she called me full of emotions and questions, I tried to help her. I can be a good womanly influence. But I can never be her mother.

When I turned fifty-two, I realized I was older than my sister would ever be. That made me sad on so many levels, but it also made me realize that one of the most important lessons we can learn in this life, as children or adults, is the power of resilience. It's never too late to develop that quality. These days when I run across old photos of my sister, I smile. I try to mention her name in almost every conversation I have with my niece and my brother-in-law. But to this day, I will stop and think, *I need to tell Shelly something*, only to remember she's gone. She should be here.

Suicide is a thief. It robs the future. We need more than hotlines and small talk to help people like my sister. Texas ranks forty-ninth among states in funding for mental health. Perhaps it should be a bit more of a priority. Until you experience mental illness firsthand, its impact is difficult to fathom. Suicide in my family? Never. No. But it happened to me. Privileged, educated, middle-class, white me. It happened to me. I know now that I can be happy again, and I am. But I am forever changed.

Respect the Lechuza

ALEX RUBIO

I grew up on the West Side of San Antonio, in the Mirasol housing projects off of El Paso Street and General McMullen Drive, near Castroville Road. I remember the Mirasol projects—my barrio, my home—with my mother, Guy Rubio. My mother was a single-parent, first-generation Super Chicana, and I'm second-generation Chicano. I think my mother's superpower was her bottomless Mexican purse, a hand-tooled leather bag embossed with an Aztec glyph of the sun god. When we went to the movies at the Cine Mexico theater on Castroville Road, she would pull all kinds of food out of that purse, like tacos, Cokes, and bags of Fritos.

My mom was very wise. Wisdom is one thing I look up to and cherish with respect. Yet I sometimes didn't listen to my mother's wise words. My *tías* and *tíos* are charged with wisdom, my cousins, not so much. Yet I consider myself one of the lucky ones because I grew up with such an amazing family and such incredible cultural stories, like the Lechuza.

Some of us have maybe never heard of the Lechuza. So, it's very strange to find out that I have quite a relationship with people across the nation who have shared their Lechuza sightings with me. The Lechuza was one of those rare birds that would totally ruin a weekend for me or cancel a trip to Corpus Christi. I would hear my mom on the phone with my *tía* saying, "I'm sorry, we have to cancel the trip to Corpus because there was a Lechuza in the tree last night," or "We're not going to the movies this weekend because I heard the Lechuza sing last night." We would have to stay in all weekend because of the Lechuza.

The Lechuza is one of those stories that becomes real after a while. It has been part of my family all my life. I also hear about her from my *tías* and *tíos* from California. They describe her as an owl, which is the literal translation from Spanish—just an owl. They describe her as a large bird with the head and torso of a female figure, red eyes, and a large wingspan. I was actually a Chicano nonbeliever until one night when it became very real. I could not imagine such a creature until I saw her.

I remember that night clearly. It was my birthday. It was three in the morning. I'd had a little too much to drink, but I couldn't make this stuff up. I was walking home from a party, and I was passing Vidaurri Park, which is still there, near the Veramendi housing project on the West Side. It started pouring rain with tremendous thunder and lightning. The only lights that were still on were at Vidaurri Park. It was one of San Antonio's rolling black-outs, and all I could see was the lightning illuminating this

dead-looking tree in the middle of the park next to the ga-
zebo. It still stands today. As I was walking by, I heard rustling in the tree. I looked up, and sure enough, it was the
Lechuza. I keep thinking of those descriptions—a large
bird, long neck, red eyes—and that was exactly what I saw.

I was frozen staring at this humongous bird that
sounded like a grackle—almost like a grackling, crackle
sound. It looked down at me with big glowing, red eyes.
When it started shifting, its wingspan spread across the
width of the tree. It was like the condor at the San Antonio Zoo. It was huge. The wings were wider than my 1964
Ford Falcon. At that moment, I remembered everything
my mother had taught me about what to do, and not do,
when you see a Lechuza. You don't throw rocks at it. You
don't cuss at it. You don't pour salt on it, as if that were
some magical evil protection barrier. You just walk away.

Well, I ran away, toward a phone booth—they actually had phone booths back then. I had one quarter in my
pocket. I called my mother, and I said, "Mama, there's a
Lechuza in the tree."

And she said, "Ah, Dios mío, oh my God."

"Whatever you do," she yelled, "don't listen to her.
Don't talk to her, and whatever she tells you, just ignore
her. Turn around and walk away."

"Mom," I said, "I'm gonna ignore her and run away!"

As I was running home that night, I could almost feel
the Lechuza flying across the sky, chasing me down, as if I

were in a true Chicano horror story—the Lechuza played by Cheech Marin, my part played by Danny Trejo, and directed by Robert Rodriguez.

That's the moment all San Antonio legends became real to me. The Donkey Lady, the Tracks, La Llorona at Our Lady of the Lake at Elmendorf Park. All very true, very true. And yet when I was young, I didn't believe my grandfathers, my thirteen *tíos* and *tías* working as migrant workers as they moved across the United States, spreading the story of how the owl is the only bird that can travel to and from the underworld to bring us messages and omens.

The Lechuza is probably one of the most misunderstood urban legends in San Antonio. She is an omen, a bird spirit totem, and my mother was wise enough to listen to her warnings. I was not at that point, but I am now.

What Are You Doing Here?

JONATHAN RYAN

"What are you doing here?" says the man standing out-side the van, looking at me like I'd never seen anyone do before—a mix of shock and pity with a touch of curiosity. It was a look that signaled to me for the first time since I'd been arrested and thrown into that van that I might be in some big trouble.

I had just wrapped up my winter holiday—a vacation in Mexico with my parents and brother—following my first semester in law school. The bus I took to get to Mexico had crossed the border in the early morning hours, and I managed to sleep through the immigration checkpoint where I should have obtained my tourist visa for Mexico. When I arrived in Guanajuato and was greeted by my fam-ily, they had some fun at my expense over the fact that I (the *lawyer*) had managed to wind up in Mexico with-out a visa. We went straight to the U.S. consulate, where I learned that in addition to having no visa to be in Mexico, my U.S. resident card (I'm Irish) had also expired. "Not to worry," the consular officer said pleasantly, before quickly adding, "but you might have some explaining to do at the border."

I had a wonderful time in Mexico, and we all but forgot about that small issue at the border. On the long ride back to the United States, our bus was stopped at a checkpoint run by the Mexican police. Men with large automatic rifles surrounded the bus while two others boarded to check everyone's documents. Watching from the back seat as they methodically approached, I imagined various humorous and disarming ways to tell them I had no visa. But when they got to me, all I could do was shrug my shoulders and smile.

In less than a minute, they had taken me and my bag off the bus, which promptly closed its doors and left. They put me in a small passenger van parked on the side of the road. After several hours, the door slid open and three more people got in: a man with two young children. A man from their bus was walking behind them, and even though I couldn't understand much I could tell that he was appealing to the cops to let the family go. That's when I saw it—or more correctly, that's when he saw me. His eyes widened, his jaw dropped, and he said, "What are you doing here?"

It was that voice, and that look, that opened my mind to the world of potential trouble I could be facing. I blurted out my parents' names and where they were just as the van door slammed shut. The man persisted and argued with the military unit outside, but they eventually escorted him back onto his already departing bus. Inside the van, the man addressed his two children in Portuguese. As he spoke, he pulled small scraps of paper out from his jacket and quickly handed some to each child. He started eating the paper while nodding his head up and down, as if to encourage the kids to do the same. With the obedience of a first communion, they followed his lead.

More time passed, and then the back door to the van opened and three teenage boys were loaded in. They weren't sitting silent and still like us, which broke the solemn atmosphere that had taken hold. Minutes later, our host got into the driver's seat and drove us away. I remember trying to create a mental log of each left and right turn, and how long in between them, until we got to our destination. It didn't work.

The detention center we eventually arrived at had many rooms: one group room that was already filled with people, which is where the three teenagers went; a single room next to that one, which was my room; and an upstairs room where the Brazilian family went. The group room was locked, but the other two rooms were unlocked so we could access an adjoining bathroom. My cell was dirty and smelly, and it was jumping with fleas, but it felt safe, and for the first time I could lie down flat.

The next morning, I was sitting in the front office of the detention center. My family had arrived, and a civil servant had been called in to work on a Sunday to process me out. I sat on that bench next to my parents, watching this man with his bright white Sunday shirt typing up the document that would deliver me safely home. I could feel that paper envelope of privilege folding around me again. Two hours and two hundred dollars later, I was on my way.

Since that day, I've reflected on what happened to me in that bus station, in that van, and in that detention center. I didn't realize it at the time, but I've never experienced such unbridled privilege as I did in that Mexican jail. I've also learned that somebody in my situation being held in the United States would definitely not get treated as well. In the years since, I've worked with people trying to live without documents. I've also learned enough to know that things probably didn't end up well for any of the people I was detained with. We were all up the same creek that day, but I had a paddle, even though I didn't know it at the time. I think about that man who looked at me from outside the van. I wish I could speak with him today.

The truth is, you didn't help me. But you tried. You spoke my language, and in that moment your small gesture was the only glint of hope I had. So, I am happy, these many years later, to answer your question: I'm still here, trying every day to be to other people what you were to me that day. As a lawyer, I can help a few of them, and they will know what I'm doing here.

Sixteen and Living in a War Zone

YARA SAMMAN

Although the patient was sedated, I could feel that his fingers were moving slightly along the table. It wasn't my first time in the OR, but it was definitely the first time I'd seen a patient awake under surgery. The room felt tense. The day wasn't much different from the other days in Syria, with bombs and missiles exploding around the hospital, but we could tell that this day would be significantly worse due to the sheer number of patients coming into the hospital.

The hospital was in an area we used to call the tangent line, or the battle line, because of all the bombs that would fall around it. It was where the two opposing groups would "meet" to finish their fight. I came from Homs, which is the city of the revolution, where the majority of the rebellion took place. The Syrian Revolution started with people who wanted change in the country, to have some basic human rights and some freedom. This was all part of the domino effect of the Arab Spring, a look toward a brighter future. The protesters, however, were met with much violence from the government side, which soon turned the peaceful revolution into a destructive and bloody civil war.

Because of the civil war, Homs was under siege for three years. The first year was probably the most difficult for all of us. I was homeschooled during that time, with little to no electricity to keep me occupied. As a bored sixteen-year-old, I decided to join my father, an orthopedic surgeon in the hospital, and volunteer in any way I could be helpful. Because of the hospital's dangerous location, a lot of people couldn't make it to work. Many couldn't leave their homes due to a mini-siege in their neighborhood.

The hospital was understaffed, to say the least, so they put me to work. Part of my job was simple—give the physicians the surgical equipment they needed, such as gloves, sanitizers, stitches....I knew it wasn't lifesaving work, but it gave me purpose in these dark times.

With the lack of staff and a war happening outside, you can imagine the environment the hospital operated under. The rooms were always filled with dust due to bombings around the hospital. We often felt the hospital shake, especially if the "battle" was outside its doors.

Halfway through one of the first surgeries I was sitting in on, I noticed the patient moving. *That's not normal, right?* I thought. The anesthesiologist explained that the patient was sedated and could not feel the majority of the pain. Since there was a huge shortage of essential anesthetic drugs, they had to ration them and could not keep him completely under. Basically, the city was under siege not just in terms of people coming in or out, but also in terms of food and medical supplies entering. Everyday necessities and basic supplies for survival had become a privilege.

I decided to go and hear the patient out. He rambled on with stories of fighting as a rebel against the dictatorship. He talked about how he wanted freedom and democracy for Syria. He spoke about his four young kids and how he wanted to see them grow up in a country that respected them and gave them their civil rights. He went on about the house he built with hard work, and his heartbreak at seeing it destroyed within seconds. He came from Baba Amr, a neighborhood at the epicenter of the fighting in 2012—now completely destroyed. I felt awe and respect for him, and for his sacrifice. I understood that his pain didn't come from his destroyed house or the surgical blade running through his skin, or even the bullet lodged in his leg. It was his fear that all his sacrifice would be in vain, that five years into the revolution, nothing would change. Unfortunately, our destiny seemed to be headed to a place far worse.

Even though my stance was one of support toward the rebels, I was very suspicious of the act of fighting itself.

When you meet violence with violence, force with force, you will eventually fall into the trap of committing atrocities, regardless of the initial intentions. Through my time in the operating room, I saw that the doctors were the true heroes. My father was the true hero. They risked their lives every day to treat the injured, whoever they were— whether it was the government side, innocent patients, or the rebel side. They went to work fully aware that if they got caught treating rebels, the government would imprison, torture, or even kill them. They continued working under the Hippocratic Oath they had taken long ago in medical school.

Aleppo is another city that was being bombed constantly. In October 2016 the last children's hospital that was supported by Doctors Without Borders was bombed. There is no humanity in what's going on, but I still have faith. The doctors I've seen in the hospital, alongside my father, have given me faith in humanity. The patient survived, but unfortunately many did not. I pray for them and for their families every day.

I hope I've given you a glimpse of life in Syria in 2016. None of us thought we would come to the point where we wouldn't have hospitals, schools, or even houses to live in. I hope that eventually the refugees living in atrocious conditions in camps will be able to go home and find a country that will support them, love them, and give them back their dignity.

Today is August 31, 2022. I am editing this story I wrote in 2016 with a heavy heart. I lived through three years of the war and watched the other seven from a safe distance. Even with the corruption Syria is facing now, I am always fighting to keep the optimism I once had in my heart. I owe it to my mother and father for leaving the country they invested their future in to ensure that my siblings and I would have a fair shot at a better life. I learned much of my resilience from them as I watched them both start over from scratch. As a medical student now, I hope to become the kind, brave, and skilled doctor my father has always been and to carry myself with the tenacity, resilience, and elegance of my mother.

A City Boy—Under Protest

JOHN PHILLIP SANTOS

The street where I live? First thing I've got to mention: there've been many. Eland. Inglewood. Hopeton. Rectory Road. Lake Place. Hopeton again. Second Avenue. Crescent. Central Park West. Lullwood. And Hopeton yet again. I've only ever lived on a street.

I'm a lifelong urbanite. I've only ever lived in cities. San Antonio, Texas; South Bend, Indiana; Oxford, England; New Haven, Connecticut; and a very long stint in Manhattitlán, New York City. But here's the thing: I'm essentially a country boy. I'm someone who has wanted to live off the grid before there was even a grid.

I wanted to live outside the cities, away from the streets, out of sight of any neighbors. In this vision, I saw a vast landscape between myself and the horizon in every direction. So, in this spirit, I'm reflecting on the street where I live in a contrarian vein.

My split identity regarding cities began in childhood. When I was growing up, we had a little ranch that my father bought with a G.I. Bill loan. There we were, every Saturday morning, going from Eland Drive in the Dellview neighborhood of San Antonio to our ranchito off of Pleasanton Road. There we found our little primeval Texas stillness—sandy riverine terrain, the Gulf Plains valley countryside that begins just south of San Anto.

We had a Shetland pony named Brown Beauty. I'd wanted a palomino, but when we went to the auction my dad told me we could only afford a Shetland pony—a very contrary and ill-tempered Shetland pony. Brown Beauty took special delight in bucking all of us into the prodigious cactus stands that dotted our ranchito.

And this question came up for me back then: the city or the country?

The world of streets or the world of dusty roads?

I was always for the dusty roads.

But I've only ever lived in cities.

As a young man, I lived many of my summers for long stints in Coahuila, staying—sometimes working—on the Sierra Madre ranch the family had there. I found a stone perch off the road into the ranch that had a seat weathered by rain and wind. At the end of late-afternoon sierra runs I'd sit on that boulder throne and gaze at the Sierra Madre sun going down behind these fantastic, jagged peaks. *That*, I thought, *was where I wanted to be, always*.

But I always found myself in cities instead.

Admittedly, I came to know that streets were places of signs and wonders. You could live near the streets to witness augurs of things to come. The first of these came in England, when I had these clichéd expectations of landing in the ancient university town of Oxford. I got to my first perch there on Rectory Road, a beautiful little tree-decked street. That morning—my first wakening—I heard the muezzin's ancient Muslim call to prayer. I'd never heard that before—a prayer, a spiritual exhortation, wafting in the wind. Later in the day, when I went off looking for the mosque, I discovered a pub in the middle of the block, the Hound and Ox. Another revelation: you could have a pub on your block. The calls to prayer and the pub would shape much of my life in the decades to come—as a journalist exploring religious communities, religious belief, traveling all around the world, and lots of time spent in pubs. So, that street in Oxford harbored a slowly unfolding revelation in my life.

And later in New York City—or in New Haven, one of the next cities—I found myself, almost every night, engaged in conversation with friends about class struggle, about arms struggle, about the struggle to get through the day. One neighbor was brought up on charges for a silver heist that was meant to send money to the militants uprising in Salvador. That ongoing world struggle shaped many of the vistas to come—the experience of the poor meeting the rich right in the middle of an old American university city.

I ultimately found my way to New York City, where I spent nearly twenty-five years. Never a "New Yorkino," I always felt myself more of a Texano in exile. But I landed there in 1984, on Second Avenue and Fourth Street, at the epicenter of what remained of the punk world, two blocks away from CBGB.

There was a nightly thieves' market on the street that opened up at twilight. I lived in a beautiful—well, an ample—basement-bunker apartment over a Korean transvestite disco where sonorous revelries continued well into the night. Nobody slept in those days, conveniently, so all of us were part of the revelry.

Walking one night on that street, on Second Avenue, those tough, colorful blocks between Saint Marks Place and Fourth Street, I came across a pile of photographs. As I started rifling through them, I found all these photographs of 1920s San Antonio: the Sunken Garden, neighborhoods, downtown streets, San Pedro Creek.

It was as if the ghost of my old city was somehow haunting the city I found myself in. The city that was then home, and yet it was just a way station between trips, between myriad streets and cities.

New York was my new hometown. But I was away for 9/11. I was in the Jemez wilderness of northwest New Mexico, in a place that's like my version of the fortress of solitude, a place I find I make my way to, intentionally or not, for escape, retreat, renewal. When I was able to make my way back to the city, there was a sense of New York being different, altered by a grievous wound, and somehow the fact that I wasn't there separated me from all those who experienced it, along with my brother, Charles.

The years dragged on. Life was changing, friends had moved away, my girlfriend lived in Copenhagen. New York had never been lonely before, but it began to be lonely. And then in August 2003, where I lived on Central Park West, with a terrace above the park, I was on the phone in the middle of the day. I was talking to my girlfriend, and I saw a plume of smoke jump up from the East River with a giant bang. About three seconds later all the lights went out.

It was the big city blackout of 2003, the biggest since 1970.

Luckily, I had shopped amply that morning, and I had a hibachi on my terrace. I called the remaining friends I had in the city to gather there. We lit a fire, we grilled steaks, mushrooms, and peppers.

When the twilight came, New York City was unlike any time I'd ever known there before. It was as if nature had reclaimed the city. There was this stillness I remembered from the ranch off of Pleasanton Road. People's voices were audible, and it was as if I were being called yet again to head out from the land of the streets to seek new havens.

I returned to San Antonio not too long after that with new love, new futures beckoning. I live today in the house I grew up in, on the street I grew up on. The second generation of Santoses, our daughter, is growing up there, walking the streets I set out from, walking our collie and chihuahua, the very same streets I set out into the world from.

There is still a sense that we're waiting for signs of that time ahead—of a place beyond the streets, a place in the countryside, whether in Texas, or Mexico, or some other part of the world.

Buried Alive

BURGIN STREETMAN

The first time I thought I was going to die, I was twelve years old. I say the first time because this was not the only time my mother put me in a life-or-death situation. My mother's name was Sally, and she came from a very wealthy southern family. About the time she graduated from college, my grandfather started getting really ill and having paranoid delusions that someone was going to kidnap his daughters, like the Lindbergh baby. He began giving all his money away, even though both of his daughters were married and out of college.

I, on the other hand, didn't grow up with a ton of money. But because my mother grew up wealthy, she raised us as if we were wealthy. We were the only kids in private school who had to wear the same outfits every day—not because it was the uniform but because I had only two outfits. I had a long-sleeve, purple Panama Jack T-shirt, back when they were cool, and I had a magenta Michael Jackson *Thriller* shirt that was a hand-me-down from my sister. Because we were always broke, Sally was always trying to come up with ways for us to get rich.

One time a man was kidnapped near where we lived and held for ransom. The family put up a large reward for anybody who had information leading to his whereabouts. Sally decided that if anybody was going to get that cash, it might as well be us.

About two months earlier she had read an article in the *Reader's Digest* about a woman who was kidnapped and buried alive. Now, no offense to the *Reader's Digest*, but this was rural South Carolina in the 1980s, and everyone, and I mean everyone, with a third-grade education read the magazine. The uncanny thing about this particular article was that it had step-by-step instructions for how the perpetrator went about burying this woman. It was illustrated with line drawings and guidelines, like the exact size and amount of tubing you'd need to siphon sufficient air into the box unit and how you have to bury the person with beef jerky and water to keep them alive.

Sally got the idea that whoever abducted this guy must have read the article too. And it wasn't just an idea, it was gospel to her. *This is what happened. This man read the article, got this idea, and went and did the same thing.* My mother started going around town and asking people, where is there a lot of soft soil? And, if you were going to dump a dead body, or bury somebody alive, where would you do it?

After lots of this type of "detective work," she narrowed it down to a little landfill just outside of town. She decided to check it out, and she decided it was a good idea to take me with her. Sally and I arrived at the landfill, which just happens to be located way off the main road, in the middle of fucking nowhere. We had to drive miles down this dirt track, deep into Carolina longleaf pine forest. The landfill was filled with old appliances, abandoned cars, and garbage and surrounded by thick woods on three sides. Now, calculating through the mind of a criminal, my mother decided we would search the wooded areas first.

Following the landfill's perimeter, we saw lots and lots of leaves. Beer cans. More leaves. A fallen tree. Some pine cones. Probably all sorts of creepy animals, but hey, we had a man to rescue, so whatever. We searched for about an hour. By that time it was getting late and I was getting tired. I just wanted to go home, and I started voicing this desire. I didn't even really know what we were supposed to be looking for. After an extended period of whining, I somehow convinced my mother to leave.

We were heading to the car when we came across a mound of dirt. It was about five inches high, maybe three feet across and six feet long. It looked like somebody might have tried to conceal it with dried leaves and branches. After further investigation, my mother produced an empty beef jerky container and a milk carton dated the week of the abduction. She was convinced this was where the guy was buried. There was no doubt in her mind that the guy was under there, so she got down on all fours and started talking into the ground.

"Hello? Hello? Is anybody down there? Hello?"

As she was doing this I heard a car approach, then a car door slam and what sounded like two men having a conversation. My mother grabbed me by the back of my neck and pulled me to the ground. "Burgin. Stay low and be quiet. *Shhhhhhhh.*"

Here we were. Two women, alone, hunched over in the darkening woods, looking for living graves in the middle of very rural nowhere circa 1980-whatever. I think at this point Sally was really starting to question her judgment. Me? I was scared shitless. She had me crawling along the ground at top speed, and I could hear the men banging around and my mother talking to herself in a frantic but hushed tone. "Shit. It's them. They've come to check on the body. We're fucked. Oh, my God. What have I done— what have I done to my baby?"

All of a sudden everything went dead silent. The guys stopped talking. They stopped walking. There was no noise at all. Silence.

It was starting to get dark. I don't know if you know anything about the ecology of South Carolina, but it's similar to Texas in that this is full-on rattlesnake, copperhead, cottonmouth feeding time of day. Even though it's technically still light out, you can't really make out what's in front of you. The Carolina pine trees are so dense that you can barely see the sky poking through. It's the kind of scary that's impossible to get away from because you're in it. It's 100 percent around you.

Just as I was starting to breathe for the first time in what seemed like forever, I heard a gun go off. And not just to go off—a bullet hit the tree trunk right behind Sally's head. Bark exploded everywhere. My mother looked at me and mouthed the word "run." I started running as fast as I could. There were bullets whizzing over my head, leaves flying all over the place, and I couldn't breathe. I was thinking, *Oh, my God, this is it, this is how I'm going to die, this is how it's going to end.* I was wondering if it was going to be too painful. I kept glancing back at Sally, who was lagging behind. "Run! Run! Save yourself!" Her hair was flying all over the place. She looked like something out of the first scene in a horror movie, and it was horrible. Plus, she wasn't running as fast as she needed to be.

We finally got to the clearing, completely out of breath. Out of the cover of the forest, our eyes adjusted to the last bit of light. I could see my mother's maroon Pontiac station wagon on the right, only a few yards away. Then we saw them on the left, these two men dressed in overalls and baseball caps. They were sitting on the back of a pickup truck and laughing. They were drinking beer and shooting at two little paper targets they'd taped up on the embankment. They must have been pretty drunk because they were missing the targets altogether.

I was looking at Sally, and she was looking at me. We were looking at the guys. And I thought, *Well, that was stupid.* Here I thought we were on the brink of death, and it's just these two guys having a fucking turkey shoot. I was twelve, so I was sort of disappointed that it wasn't as romantically tragic as it might have been.

About a week later, the family of the kidnapped man made a deal and secured an exchange with the kidnappers. The newspaper reported that the family dumped the money under a bridge, just like in the movies. The kidnappers came and took the money, leaving nobody behind. The kidnappers and the man who was kidnapped were never heard from again.

Sally and I, that day in the woods, immediately left and went to a gas station, where she cried and told the attendant the whole story. She called the sheriff from the pay phone outside. I could hear them laughing through the line as she tried to explain the mound and the beef jerky and the article from the *Reader's Digest.*

What you saw out there was nothing. It was probably a dog's grave.

Every time I think about this story, I remember how Sally and I told it so many times. Dozens and dozens and dozens of times. Sometimes in storytelling it's hard to differentiate between what really happened and what you've elaborated on over the years. But I am telling you, if you had asked my mother, until the very day she died she would have told you that guy was still out there, rotting behind the landfill.

Fake Heads and Wonder

WHITLEY STRIEBER

The experience I wrote about in my 1987 book, *Communion*, is familiar to many. People think of it as an alien abduction story, but it is actually about an enigmatic human experience that science does not yet understand. I have always lived life in a state of wonder, and that began right here in San Antonio, not far from Taylor Street. In the summer of my tenth or eleventh year, my mother took me to the Witte Museum with the thought that I would enjoy wandering around while she attended a meeting there.

She was exactly right. I loved that place. My great-grandmother's Pierce-Arrow was in the automobile exhibit, which was always fun to see, but more important, by far—in my boyhood's wondering eyes—was the exhibit of two shrunken heads.

I gazed into the glass case, wondering, as I always did, *Were their lips sewed closed when they were alive or after they'd been executed and shrunk?* As I ruminated on this question, a voice floated down from above: "Little boy, what are you doing?"

I looked up, and there stood a tall woman in a long white dress, looking dangerously angelic. Strapping on my best manners, I answered, "Ma'am, I'm looking at the shrunken heads."

"You should be looking at the stars," she said. "What is your name?"

Like any little boy being confronted by an adult with unknown motives, I thought, *uh-oh*. I had to answer, of course. I said, "My name is Whitty Strieber."

"Very well," she said, and swept off into the museum.

Now, an aside about the shrunken heads. We'll get back to the lady in just a moment. Forty years later, my wife, Anne, and I had moved back to San Antonio. I was on a search for my past. What came out of it was the book *The Secret School*, an exploration of a boy's dreams and imaginings and how they were woven into the magic of the life I lived here.

One afternoon we were having coffee with a friend, Mary Kargl. I have always loved the story of the shrunken heads, and I was telling it to Mary as a lead-in to the wonderful tale I am about to tell you. I ended my description of them with the question, "I wonder what became of them?"

Mary immediately said, "Would you like to see them?"

I was astonished. "See them? They've been gone from the museum for years."

"I've got them right here," she said.

I thought, *What? It's impossible.*

"Let me show you." She got up, walked across the living room, and opened a drawer in a tall sideboard. There they were.

"Where in the world did you get the shrunken heads, Mary?"

"My husband donated them to the museum many years ago," she said, "and it turns out that they're fakes. They're actually made of gutta-percha, so they were deaccessioned."

Apparently, counterfeit shrunken heads were manufactured by tribes in the Amazon for sale to tourists. They were convincing when I was ten, and I have to say that at age fifty, this was still true.

Let's get back to the Witte Museum and the mid-1950s, and a little boy who was about to touch the edge of wonder. My mother came and collected me, and on the way home she said, "Aline Carter has invited you to her house to go to her observatory on the roof and look through her telescope."

I was awed. I'd never looked through a telescope before, let alone been in an observatory. My father had bought me a home planetarium, and I used to turn out the lights in my room and switch it on, watch the grandeur of the sky parading across my ceiling, then go outside, climb up on the roof, and name all the constellations I could find.

Aline Carter had been the poet laureate of Texas and was also an astronomer. In her extraordinary and selfless life, she taught astronomy at the Witte, taught Sunday school at Saint Mark's Episcopal Church, and worked with inmates at the jail and the state hospital. She also played the harp. In my world, she was a mystery, a legendary figure. One saw her being driven around by a chauffeur in a big black limousine. She had married local attorney Henry Champe Carter when she was twenty-four and he was fifty-five. After he died she continued wearing clothes of the kind he had loved seeing her in most. She would sweep about in flowing white chiffon. Other boys had reported that there was a glass elevator in her house and that the house had its own chapel inside.

We drove to the Carter house, which I recall as being enormous. If you ever go to it, you'll see that it is indeed a magnificent mansion. We went to the front door and were let in. To my right was a small round room with a harp in it. I headed for that, and my mother immediately said, "Don't you touch that." She knew me too well. Across from the harp room was a low doorway with an inscription over it: "Be still, and know that I am God."

Mrs. Carter came downstairs and took me up a grand staircase, up another stairway, and then up a third stairway. We emerged on the roof, and there was the whole firmament; in those days, from downtown San Antonio, you could see the whole sky in all its grandeur.

She took me into the observatory, where there was another inscription: "When I behold Thy Work, Oh God."

"Would you like to see a planet?" she said.

"Yes," I said. "I would like to see a planet."

She guided me to put my eye up to the telescope, and I saw the most elegant and beautiful thing I had ever seen to that day in my life. I will never forget it. It was Saturn hanging there with her rings, shuddering slightly. I was amazed at how beautiful it was. *It was real*, I thought, *it was really there, right now*. Then she said, "What other planet would you like to see?"

I thought of the *War of the Worlds* movie and all the flying saucer stories in the newspaper, and I said Mars.

She showed me Mars, a pink speck with a white polar cap that you could just make out, which for me made it vividly real. *Another world right here*, I thought, *right before my eyes*.

In that moment, the universe opened up to me. Ever since, the wonder of its vastness, its mystery, and the mystery of the human mind that can taste of that wonder have been the center of my journey in life.

Dark Was the Night

BARBARA S. TAYLOR

In medical school, they teach you how to say the scary things, like:

The test showed that you have HIV.

The results of the biopsy are back, and the cancer is spreading.

These are terrifying things to say, horrible to hear, things I hope never to have to say again. But I will.

Most people think saying scary things rolls off doctors. Trust me, they don't. I'm going to tell you about a time when I was really, truly scared.

The first time I met Robert, I disliked him. It wasn't his fault—I didn't like him before I actually met him. (By the way, Robert is a completely made-up name that is as far from my patient's as I can imagine. I've also changed some of the details of this story to protect everyone's identity.)

I was in my first year of an infectious diseases fellowship. It was late in the afternoon of a long day, and my pager seemed to go off every thirty seconds. I had a two-month-old at home and a bunch of patients left to see. It wasn't that hard to feel sorry for myself.

My boss pages me and says, "There's some newly diagnosed guy in the intensive care unit who won't tell his partner he has HIV. Stop by there and sort him out, because he's going to be your clinic patient. If he makes it out of the ICU, which doesn't look super likely at this point."

I slog over to the ICU to "sort out" my future patient. There are a lot of reasons not to tell your partner you have HIV. Most of them bad. So, already I'm not a big fan of Robert.

I get to his cubicle, and there he is, the only person in the ICU not hooked up to a ventilator—a small, exhausted-looking young man lost in a sea of bedsheets, warming blankets, beeping IV poles, and the little booties that inflate and deflate to keep you from getting blood clots. I hold out my hand, still cold from the hand sanitizer, and introduce myself, but when he takes my hand, his is so cold that it shocks me. I jerk back a little bit. He winces.

"I'm going to be your doctor once you're better and leave the hospital," I say.

He looks up at me sideways like he sees right through my whole Pollyanna act.

"I work here in the HIV clinic."

He winces again. I decide to get it over with.

"I know the doctors here have been talking to you about this, but it's very important that you tell people about your diagnosis," I say. "It will help them support you. And anyone you've had sex with over the past five years or so needs to know so they can be tested and get treatment if they need it."

He looks down at his toes. "I can't tell my fiancée."

"You need to tell her," I say.

Here it comes, I think. The excuses. All the reasons now is not the convenient time—she's got a lot on her plate, she won't be able to handle it, she'll freak out on him.

There's a long pause, and those booties deflate again.

"I know I should. I will. It's just…I'm supposed to work so she can go to school. I'm supposed to be the provider. If I die, who will help pay her tuition? Who will care for her?"

He looks at me as if I have the answers to these unanswerable questions, and I realize that he's not avoiding the issue; he just doesn't want to leave her. He feels responsible.

Suddenly, all the frustration I feel about how there's no way I'll be home before nine and how I've gotten three pages in the past three minutes goes away. I think about what it would be like to have to go home and tell my spouse I have HIV, and my heart breaks a little.

"You're not going to die," I say. Which, of course, is something you are never, ever supposed to tell an ICU patient who is actively dying at that moment. They teach us that in medical school too.

For the next few months Robert and I worked together on him not dying. He was so sick—his whole body seemed to be giving up on him. He weighed eighty pounds, he lost his hair, he took mountains of pills, threw them up, and then took more. His fiancée stuck by him the whole time. She bore the news of his diagnosis, kept her chin up, and helped him take his meds. He started to get better.

Then, almost six months after I met him, he came into the clinic looking like death again. He was an off-gray color and too weak to walk. All of his symptoms had returned. I had to stick his toothpick arms twice when I drew his blood to get a vein large enough. I paced in the hallway, waiting for the results.

And then they came: his potassium was two.

That's low. As in, inconsistent with your heart continuing to beat low. I walked into the room and told Robert and his fiancée that he was headed back to the ICU. They knew me pretty well by then, so I couldn't really hide how terrified I was.

I remember thinking, *If he dies, I don't think I can keep being a doctor. I'm not good enough. There's something I missed. It will be my fault that this amazing man isn't around to support his family, that this phenomenal woman is alone.*

This is the truly terrifying thing they don't prepare you for during medical training. The feeling that maybe there was something you could have done to prevent death, injury, pain, suffering, and you've failed.

But I'm still a doctor. I didn't quit that day—or any of the other days since when I've felt that way.

And Robert didn't die. In fact, he's great. I know this because this summer, ten years after I met him, I danced at his wedding. I remember Robert and his fiancée smiling at each other through tears while they exchanged rings, and that feeling helps keep the dark away.

From High Finance to High-Wire Act

MICHAEL TAYLOR

The story of my big break starts in January 2006. I was in Richard's office, fifth floor, Fifth Avenue, Manhattan. "What can I do for you?" he said.

"Well, as you know," I said, "I'm raising money for my distressed fixed-income fund."

"How much do you need?"

"Well, I calculated if I could get to ten million dollars, that would—"

"That's done!" he said. "And there's more where that came from. What else? What happens next?"

"Oh, well, actually, what happens is in about three weeks I'll bring you a prospectus for you to sign." What I didn't say, of course, is that I needed the lawyer to write the documents, because Richard was my first investor. "In fact, if you don't mind I'm just going to ask for probably a million dollars because as I ramp—"

"A million dollars? Don't even bring the documents."

That was my big break. Two years earlier, in 2004, I'd quit my job at Goldman Sachs. I had this theory—genius idea, actually—that we were creating a lot of debt and there would be a debt reckoning, that there was a blowup coming, and I might be able to buy debt at pennies on the dollar and make a profit for investors. How did I get this genius idea? I would say we all knew. I worked in the mortgage bond department of Goldman Sachs, and this was not a closely held secret. I was a bond salesman. Along with the rest of the team I sold the alphabet soup of products that later became known as Weapons of Mass Financial Destruction—CMBS, RMBS, IOS, POs and, if you've seen *The Big Short*, the dreaded CDOs. I had started this business two years earlier, but in Richard's office I finally had my break, and I have to tell you, if you've never experienced this, it feels really good. I mean, I am Kate Winslet at the bow of the ship, Leonardo DiCaprio is behind me, I am flying. I raised ten million bucks in five minutes. That's my big break.

Would you like to hear about the bust? I bet you would.

Fast-forward two years. It was 2008, and my fund had grown at a good clip. I was raising money—about $1 million a month—from high-net-worth folks and institutions. But by now the chairs on the ship deck were starting to move. I'll give you a few scenes from how that year went for me. Bear Stearns went under that spring; Lehman Brothers, AIG, Fannie Mae, and Freddie Mac were still around, but you know what's coming next.

My own experience started with Jeff Zavada. He runs a home improvement business in a small town in Illinois.

He owed my fund $700,000, which should have been a perfectly good debt owed to me, because he owned buildings and equipment and he'd had $5 million in revenue two years prior. This was good—until he called in the spring and said, "I have zero revenue, and I'm not paying anymore." In 2008, you may recall, nobody could get home equity loans or lines of credit, so Jeff's revenue base had gone from $5 million to zero. Eventually I liquidated some of the buildings and equipment for about $50,000. But that was the first big loss in my fund.

I started calling my investors. One in particular stood out. When I called Walter to let him know about the write-down in the fund, at first he said what I had expected, which was, "Send all my money back." What I didn't expect was this: "You're the worst," he said. "You are absolutely terrible at what you do. I hope your wife is better at what she does than you are at what you do."

Walter had never met my wife. And while I know he is a complete asshole, the truth of his statement stuck with me. It stuck for the next four years. I was terrible at what I did.

I'll give you one more scene. George Noga owed my fund $200,000. Very successful businessman, perfect credit. He'd paid this note down, and he had $3 million net worth in his retirement account. He owned a big house in Florida. I remember the morning he called because I had the stomach flu. I'm already not feeling so good, and my head is a little woozy. He tells me he's declaring bankruptcy and I'll be getting none of the $200,000. How can that be? Well, he's a very clever businessman. He's what we call "bankruptcy proof." He sent a letter from his accountant stating that none of the retirement accounts and none of the home equity had to be paid to his creditors; he could keep it all in bankruptcy. The problem wasn't the $200,000 he was stiffing me with; it was the $2.5 million he owed a different bank. He was keeping all of it.

Between that news, the stomach flu, and what would clearly be the end of my fund, I decided to take a walk and try to clear my head. I want you to picture it: finance guy walking down the street in Manhattan in his button-down shirt and khakis, and as my fund was closing my bowels were opening up, and I literally shit myself walking down the street.

A postscript to the George Noga story: I flew down to Florida to find out what happened. He picked me up in his late model Lexus. "How did you get that?" I said. And he said, "I leased this the week before we declared bankruptcy because I knew I couldn't afterward. Please don't tell my personal assistant—or the guys at the golf club—what's happened. It's kind of a secret that I've declared bankruptcy." So, he was stiffing people.

The fund was over. I needed to make more calls. People like Richard got most of their money back. The worst was the calls to the first people who believed in me, including one of my best friends growing up, a couple of guys from college who work in finance, my favorite friend from Goldman, my mom, and my eighth-grade English teacher. Those were not good calls to make. Essentially, for the next four years, I carried Walter's voice in my head, that I was terrible at what I did. That's how the bust felt.

I'll just end on a recovery note. My wife noticed that the most important voice in my head was Walter's. For my fortieth birthday she asked sixteen people, friends and family, to write a letter saying what they thought about me, as a kind of a counterweight to Walter's voice. We bound that book—*Letters to Michael*. There was a passage my brother wrote that helped a lot: "Just know that we love you and have all the confidence in the world that you will eventually see again the greatness and goodness we all see in you." If my house were on fire and all the humans had to leave in a hurry, this is the only thing I'd grab on my way out.

Miseducation Blues

KIRSTEN THOMPSON

I can honestly say that I can't remember a time when the undercurrent of racism was absent from my life. When taking inventory of personal history, people tend to employ the expression "hindsight is twenty-twenty." What I have learned is that intuition is just as sharp, keen, and informed in its own vision.

I won't pretend that racism reared its ugly head at every waking moment or that each experience was blatant. Rather, it always seemed to be in the ether, lurking about. It informed so much of how we existed without ever being called by name. Whether that was in expectation of our behavior as children (because the standard is different) or if we could pass through certain towns, depending on the time of day or night. Sometimes it was a matter of watching my parents being treated differently by their peers. Again, not every instance was an in-your-face affront; there were times where it was simply palpable, delivered in condescending words and tones or haughty looks. Or those menacing ones that say "you really shouldn't be here."

One particular experience delivered a gut punch to me. I still remember it vividly thirty years later. It was summer

1991, and my mother, two sisters, and I had just moved to San Antonio from a small town outside of Houston. I was elated because I was going into junior high. In my child's mind, junior high was basically tantamount to high school—therefore, I was entering the wonderful world of adulthood. I was eager to make friends in a new city and excited to learn. I knew that there would be bigger libraries with more books and that my saxophone and I would be in a much larger band.

In my second year, I met one of my absolute favorite teachers. She spoke to us in a way most teachers didn't speak to their students. She allowed us room to think and process information and come to our own conclusions, rather than tell us what they should be. She was tall and elegant, and worldly, and she had impeccable diction. I admired her greatly. I enjoyed attending her class because I always got extra credit opportunities, which I relished. I remember being delighted to learn that my class grade was often over one hundred. I valued the way she taught and, most importantly, how she interacted with me.

One day I noticed that more Black girls were being enrolled into the school. This was significant because the student body was predominantly white and Latino with a few Black children sprinkled in. I didn't really belong to a clique. I got along with everyone, especially the students in my theater arts class. We were allowed to be unfettered and imaginative, and the world seemed so full of possibility and magic.

In my seventh-grade year, several military families moved in. I was thrilled because I was starting to see more girls who looked like me. We all introduced ourselves in that unassuming way kids do, and we hit it off. It was wonderful! It wasn't long before we began to sing and harmonize in the hallways, make up little dances outside on the blacktop, and giggle in huddles while walking to class. It's almost embarrassing now, but we even dressed alike on certain days. I had found a unique comfort and kinship with these girls.

One day that favorite teacher looked in my direction as she entered the lunchroom. We made eye contact, but it was awkward. I didn't know what it was; I just knew it was a little bit different from how we normally connected. She didn't smile and, for whatever reason, neither did I. It felt weird, but I didn't think anything of it. I just waved, and she sort of nodded and then left the cafeteria. Because I had her class later in the day, it was several hours before I saw her again. After class she pulled me aside and said, "Kirsten, you have so much potential, you are so smart, you're one of my favorite students."

"Thank you!" I exclaimed.

Then she lowered her voice and said, "But I want you to be really careful about who you're hanging out with."

Now I had a very conservative, strict upbringing. There was no hanging out for me at the time. I didn't know what she was talking about, so I asked what she meant. Her response was: "Well, I noticed you've been spending time in the hallways with different kids—a crowd you normally don't associate with." The only difference I could think of was these three girls. She said, "You have so much potential. I just don't want you to ruin it."

I sat there for a minute, utterly dumbfounded. My confusion slowly turned to sadness, because I really liked my new friends. Why should I stop associating with them? Then my sadness turned into anger. I was livid. It was like a lightning strike. At that moment, I realized that my favorite teacher didn't think I should hang around those Black girls and that doing so would somehow mess up my potential.

I never looked at her the same way after that day. She always insisted I was her most promising student, but I stopped caring. Every once in a while, I get that same knot in my stomach when I'm in a similar position because those experiences tend to stay with a person. There are people who want to associate or align with you as long as you aren't "too Black." Or only if they can tokenize you.

A friend of mine recently said on social media that racism is like that toxic friend who's always in the middle of every argument in a circle of friends, and when you start to examine it you realize you don't know what anyone's arguing about, or what the issue is, because that toxic friend will be there and will show whatever face is necessary. The face I was shown that day was racism. It was subtle, but discouraging a young child from hanging out with other children who haven't done anything wrong, just because there's "too many" of you together—that's a problem!

When I first shared this story publicly, I remember saying, "Best believe, if I ever run into that teacher I will be sure to tell her how she made me feel that day." But in the nearly two years that have passed, I have come to terms with the fact that I don't need to be the one to educate this woman or people like her. The onus seems to always be on people of color to correct and challenge racism, subtle or otherwise.

Well, I am not carrying that assignment any longer. Racism is not a problem that was created by people who look like me, and it's not our job to fix it. If and when we choose to speak up, protest, and lobby for change, that is our right. But we aren't obligated to provide free education to those who have that deficit.

Young children who are on the receiving end especially should never have that obligation foisted upon them.

Don't Mess with a Theater Major

CLAY UTLEY

In fall 1999 I was a freshman theater major at a college in Abilene, Texas. Y2K and the end of the world were floating out there on the horizon. My first couple of months of college were amazing—I had just been cast in a student film project for the Halloween film festival. We were scheduled to make our horror short film late on a Friday night in the local cemetery. Back in October 1999, no one I knew had a cell phone. Literally no one. And in the days before cell phones, making plans took more effort. You had to plan ahead. You had to coordinate schedules. At lunch on Friday in the dining hall, the director of the film, Jonathan, tells me the plan for filming that night. "Just wait in your dorm room," he says. "I'll call and tell you where to meet." I'm like, "Awesome."

That night I'm waiting by the phone. I'm waiting. I'm waiting. I'm waiting. I get bored. I walk down the hall to my buddy Beau's room. Beau is also a freshman theater major, and we do what college freshmen do on a Friday night. We start watching a movie, playing video games. All of a sudden the phone in Beau's room rings, and this is the conversation I hear: "Oh, yeah... Awesome. Yeah, you know, I'm not doing anything. Yeah, I'll be right there. Okay, bye."

Beau gets up and starts to leave, and I say, "Dude! Where are you going?"

"Oh, man, that was Jonathan," he says. "He's filming a short film tonight. He said he called your room and you weren't there, so he offered me the part."

"Beau," I say, "you didn't think to tell him, 'Clay is sitting right here, let me pass the phone to him'?"

"No, that didn't cross my mind." And he walks out of the room to film my movie! I'm sitting alone, fuming and furious, my evening ruined. It crosses my mind to destroy my friend's room, but I don't—I have some self-control. As I start walking down the hall, I begin to form a plan. With every step I take, my enthusiasm for this plan grows. By the time I reach my room, I think, *This is the perfect way to spend a Friday night.* I open my closet and go to the costume section. Yes, as an eighteen-year-old I had a costume section in my closet. As an adult, I also have a costume section in my closet. I pull out this costume from Spencer's, a head-to-toe flowing black robe with a faceless black hood. It's like Ghostface from the *Scream* movies but without the face. It looks like a dementor or a Nazgûl, and I think to myself, *What a great idea.*

Beau told me exactly where the film crew was meeting. I pull out my 007 skills and tail them all the way to the cemetery, and they are none the wiser. I watch them park along this dirt road and climb a six- or eight-foot chain-link fence. I drive to the other side of the cemetery, hop the same fence, and get into position. I put on my costume and scope out their location, right in the middle of the cemetery beneath a big tree. They're setting up the lights, getting the camera ready, talking about the script. *This is perfect*, I think. I crawl on my hands and knees until I'm about two hundred feet away and wait behind a large tombstone. After a few minutes I think, *Okay, let's test this out.*

I rise from behind the tombstone like I'm rising up from the earth itself. I walk about ten feet and collapse behind another tombstone and wait for a reaction. Nothing. *They probably couldn't see me*, I think—cemeteries aren't known for their excellent lighting in the middle of the night. I rise from behind the tombstone again, walk about ten feet, collapse behind another tombstone. Then I hear Beau say, "Uh, guys, I literally just saw, like, a figure over there, and it disappeared." Conversation breaks out. Someone says, "Dude, we're filming at a cemetery in the middle of the night. We're literally surrounded by dead bodies. Your mind is playing tricks on you, man. Let's focus on the task at hand."

This is just what I was hoping for. Let's build the tension. I wait about thirty seconds and do it again. I rise from behind the tombstone, trying to make my five-foot-eight frame look as big as possible. This time I walk toward the group and collapse behind another tombstone. And then another voice: "You guys, Beau is right!" It's one of the actresses. "I saw this big black figure, and it—it was right there, and it went behind a tombstone!" The conversation escalates. The film crew murmurs, "Okay, what did you see? Where was it? Who was it? *Where* was it? Which tombstone? Should we go investigate? Should we run away?"

While they're deciding, I jump up from behind the tombstone, spread my arms as wide as I can, and charge at them full speed. All hell breaks loose. One of the girls lets out a scream that would make a Scream Queen in a horror movie jealous. Somebody knocks over the lights. They're grabbing the stuff, they don't know what to do, and somebody yells, "Let's get to the cars!" And then they start running. But the thing is, they forgot there was a six- or eight-foot chain-link fence between them and the cars.

I don't know if you've ever seen someone scared out of their mind try to climb a chain-link fence, but it's pretty comical. Their feet are slipping and sliding, their hands— they can't get a hold of the fence. That's when I realize I'm going to catch up to them. My plan didn't account for this—to be beat up on a Friday night by a bunch of theater majors. I dive behind a tombstone. Everybody makes it over the fence, except this one actress, Shae. She's having so much trouble. Here's what I do: I stand up, let out a huge guttural scream, and charge her at full speed. She begins screaming her head off, and one of her friends has to help her make it over the fence.

Everyone starts to get in the cars, and I realize they're going to leave. They're not going to know it was me who terrorized them. I want credit for this—they cannot leave before I get credit for this! I pull off my mask, and I'm like, "Hey, guys, it's me, Clay, your friend, the disgruntled theater major. I just—I came here just to scare you and kind of mess up your movie because I was frustrated I lost my part."

One by one, they get out of the cars, and that's when reality sets in. They are not doing well. Beau looks like he's lost a few years off his life. Jonathan, the director, is as white as a sheet, like on the verge of hyperventilating. And Shae has literally been crying—I know this because tears of makeup are streaked down her face. I am at a loss for words. And I'm thinking to myself, *What—what do I say?* "Hey, guys," I blurt out, "I'm sorry. I just was a little upset, and I wanted to scare you. Hope you're okay."

The most amazing thing is they weren't that upset at me. Either they were able to find the humor in the idea of being terrified by a madman while filming a horror film in a cemetery, or more likely, they were just glad I wasn't a real serial killer. I imagine they felt incredibly lucky to be alive.

Here's a pearl of wisdom for you: don't mess with a theater major, because you never know what we have hanging in our costume closet.

Baddest Drug Dealer Undone

CRISTINA VAN DUSEN

Jay came to the Healy-Murphy Center as a freshman. Healy-Murphy is a tiny school on the East Side of San Antonio that helps kids. It helps kids who are gang members or have had other run-ins with the law. It helps kids who have trouble with drugs or alcohol, who have been kicked out of other schools, who are pregnant, or who have children. Healy-Murphy helps these kids by giving them plenty of opportunities to get high school right.

Jay was preceded at Healy-Murphy by an older brother, and like any younger sibling he wanted to distance himself from the many stories about his brother—who was a scary, violent kid—and make his own name. Though he had no charisma, he was already one step ahead of the game. As I said, he came as a freshman—but not only as a freshman, as a first-time freshman, which at Healy-Murphy is a big deal. He came two classes ahead of the game in math. He could read above grade level. He could process information and apply it, and he could understand and calculate interest rates better than most adults I know. At the time, his goal in life was to become the baddest drug dealer on the East Side. He calculated the start-up costs of his dream business and determined that it was far more profitable than going to college. This boy was all about the numbers. But though he lived it every day, he had not yet learned how to quantify human misery, or really, anything other than cash. He had no regard for education whatsoever. As far as he was concerned, teachers were low-paid losers who settled for mediocrity. To Jay, they deserved their low status.

That was his view of the world the year we met.

At the time, I was the Healy-Murphy nurse, and as part of my duties I taught health classes and parent education classes. Jay was in one of my health classes. Early in my time at the school, one of the kids said to me, "Miss, if you don't lock your purse up, if I get hard up for Pampers, I'm going to steal your wallet." So, about a year and a few months into my tenure at Healy-Murphy, my purse remained locked up in a drawer, but my phone did not. It was old and boxy—you know, the unbreakable kind. We'd moved past the era of flip phones, and we had slide phones, so my phone had zero cool appeal and no street value whatsoever. It was safe.

Jay at the time was a difficult kid. He was more guarded and layered than Shrek. He guarded himself with impenetrable logic. He used it to shield himself from the world. He came up with loopholes and arguments that nobody else could see.

Looking back, it's almost sad that his biggest mistake was mundane and impulsive.

In early October of the year we met, my mother, who had been living with cancer for nearly a decade, was hospitalized in Tyler, Texas, after a round of chemotherapy destroyed her immune system. The weekend before, our family had gone up to see her. We'd all worn paper gowns and masks, and we tried to make light of the situation, teasing her about her lips—they'd swollen with the rest of her. We tried to ignore the fact that her body was failing. Her urine was dark and scant. Her lungs were filling with fluid instead of oxygen. During that visit, what she wanted most was to be able to get up, to get away from the bed and the tubing and get into the shower for a good long time. She was so tired of the bed baths.

The Monday after our visit was basically like any other Monday. I called my mother at lunchtime, and then again in the evening—briefly so my dad could visit with her when he got home from work. That night, her oxygen levels and the swelling were worse. Tuesday morning, my phone sat atop my desk, volume on high in case the hospital called. Jay and a friend of his were in fine form that day—they were extremely unsettled. They had a purple Bic lighter that they kept tossing back and forth. Then one of them lit it. I walked over and took it from Jay, who was holding it at that moment. As I locked it in the purse drawer, I could smell marijuana on the lighter. Both boys complained to no end, but soon they quieted down and I was able to resume health class.

At lunchtime, the students filed out of the clinic building, leaving me in peaceful silence. I sat at my desk and reached for my phone. But it wasn't there. A panic and numbness I had never experienced before took over my body, and I watched myself, like a spectator, as I went from student to student, asking them, "Do you know who took my phone? Do you know where my phone is?" I'm pretty sure they all knew who had it, but they wouldn't budge. They all kept absolutely silent.

When I got home that evening, I was able to use my landline. My mom had been intubated and admitted to intensive care. The nurse I spoke with told me that my mom had tried to reach me several times. She desperately wanted to talk to me. I never heard her voice again.

I spent the next three weeks sitting at her bedside, talking to her, and watching her die. In the months that followed my mother's death, my life was a complete fog. It was such a deep fog that I cannot tell you with any certainty whether Jay stopped coming to school of his own volition or because we kicked him out. Either way, the break was extremely good for both of us. By the time he reapplied and was readmitted to the school, he was near graduation; he'd matured a bit. He couldn't keep eye contact with me for long, and I'm not entirely sure he trusted completely that I would take care of him as a nurse. But over the course of the year, some of the layers peeled off, and I was able to see the boy beyond the wiliness and shrewdness. As for me, I had begun to heal, and I could look back at the phone incident not without pain, but without bitterness. This boy had not taken my phone out of malice. He was just evening the score. He was taking something of mine because I had taken something of his. I don't know if he knew his theft denied me the chance to talk with my mother for the last time.

In one of his English classes, he wrote an illustrated poem about my role at the school. He framed it and brought it to me, along with an apology and a confession. I didn't know this at the time, but the assignment was crafted by Sister Mary, who not only taught English but shepherded souls. She made this assignment shortly after Jay confided in her that he had been feeling guilty about the phone incident for a while.

Jay graduated from high school a few years ago. He's neither a drug kingpin nor a college grad. He makes pizza pies on the near East Side.

Pilgrims Lost on the Journey

EDDIE VEGA

My friend Derek could have an adventure going from point A to point B, even if point B was only ten feet away. We were part of a youth group traveling to Denver to see the pope for World Youth Day in 1993. We had to join a group from another town—I'm from McAllen, Texas—so we met up with one from Edinburg, because our group was too small.

The Edinburg group had a youth minister, while ours had moved on to get a real job somewhere else. She was a young lady named Jennifer, a college student in her early twenties. I'm not really sure she had a grasp of the situation, that she was going to be caring for twenty-five teenagers on a journey halfway across the country to be with another half a million teenagers.

Jennifer was a little strict on the trip, and that annoyed us. At each stop, when we were still on the bus, she'd say, "We're going to stop for twelve minutes. If you're not on the bus, you're going to miss going to Denver. Your parents will have to pick you up in Lubbock!" Or wherever we were. As a seventeen-year-old, I really didn't care for rules, much less for this person who wasn't much older than me telling me what to do.

We got to Denver, and at the welcome ceremony on the first evening we were seated next to a group from Spain. John Paul II was sixty yards away. We were at Mile High Stadium—right there on the grass, on the field, and the pope was in the end zone. He started speaking in English, and my Spanish friends complained that they couldn't understand what he said. I translated for them because I was a nice guy, but apparently John Paul II also knew Spanish, so he repeated everything in Spanish. Anyway, when it came time for the roll call of nations, the Spaniards brought me with them. They said I could be an honorary Spaniard. I was there saying, you know, "Juan Pablo Segundo, te quiere todo el mundo" like the rest of the Spaniards.

The highlight of the trip was a fifteen-mile walk from the state capitol to Cherry Creek State Park, which they would close down in the evening for security reasons before having mass with the pope the next morning. Normally it'd be a fifteen-mile hike, but it's a religious thing, so they called it a pilgrimage. That sounds like a long distance, and it is, but when you're seventeen and you're on God-high, you can do anything, even at a mile high. They told us to stay together. Previously they'd told us to either wear all the same shirts or carry the same flag when we were walking. Jennifer opted for the flag, so a week before our trip we decorated pink cloths and attached them to wooden dowels, and we all had flags.

That was stupid. You can wear a shirt, but you have to carry a flag, and nobody wants to do that for more than maybe three or four minutes. Nevertheless, we started walking, and within the first twenty or thirty minutes we finished the first mile as a group. Then all of a sudden we split apart. But it was okay; we could still see the rest of the group ahead. I could see three or four flags still going, but then that group split—like cell division. It was like watching mitosis. They kept going, but it was all right. We all knew where we were headed; when you're seventeen, you know exactly where you're going. I had a badge that told me where in the state park I needed to be that evening, so it was all cool.

I walked with my friend Charlie, and they said, you're doing great, you've gone one mile. I was like, man, this is awesome. We'd walk a little more, and they'd say, you're doing great, you've gone two miles. I thought, *Man, we're going to have lunch at the state park, it's awesome.* We started walking a little slower, but still, we got to three miles, four miles, five miles. We got to about seven miles, and they said, hey, you're halfway there. And I thought, *Man, we're going to have a late lunch at the park.*

We were still doing a good job, and at the next mile they said, you're halfway there! And I thought, *Seven, eight, well, you know, it's an odd number, okay*. At nine miles, they said, you're doing great, you're halfway there! And I thought, *Well, maybe we missed a mile back somewhere. We're not exactly sure where we are*. We arrived at about ten miles, or what we thought was ten miles, and they said, hey, you're doing great, it's just five more miles. And then we'd go another mile and they'd say, hey, you're doing great, it's just five more miles. It was about five more miles for the next ten miles.

At first, you're a little upset, because you ask how much longer, and they say "five more miles!" with these happy faces, and we're like, yeah, whatever, no, it's not. After a while, though, you get delirious, and because it's a great big joke and the whole crowd is moving together, somebody would yell, "How much longer?" Everybody would say, "Five more miles!"

It turns out it was twenty-five miles. They had measured the distance as the crow flies, but the crow was drunk or something, because it went in a serpentine path and it was a lot longer than we anticipated. We picked up more and more members of our original group. We'd see them on the side of the road, and we'd be like, come on, come on, you can do it, let's go. There were people there from all over the world, from Italy and Chile and Australia. They would ask what country we were from, because we didn't look like some of the other Americans, and we'd say Texas. They responded with, yeah! Texas!

We finally got to the campground. It was darker by then, maybe dusk. We were dreamy about it. *Oh, we're gonna camp out under the stars, on this mountain in Denver.* Then the temperature dropped forty degrees in eight minutes. It takes eight months for that to happen in the Valley, so the whole romantic under-the-stars thing was gone—we were freezing cold.

We found some members of our group in one of the hospital tents. We got with them, and by the next morning we had everybody—except Derek. Derek was still missing. The crowd started telling us these horror stories, like the previous day somebody had died, apparently of dehydration or exhaustion or exertion. And four babies were born—I think three boys named John Paul and a girl named Kaitlyn probably, because it was the nineties. Then we had our breakfast, had our morning prayer, had a snack, and then finally had mass with the pope. We prayed for lots of intentions, including finding Derek.

When it was over, we walked toward our bus, and from the side of a hill I heard my name in Spanish, which only my mom calls me. That is, my mom and my fellow countrymen call me that, because it was my Spanish friends—I mean, compatriots—who were there and we got to hang out with them for a while. This was kind of a miracle in itself, because once you saw somebody among half a million people, you never saw them again, and here we were seeing them on our last day.

Finally, we got on the bus—in silence, because the next stop was the hospital, where they were taking all the other survivors and refugees of this event. Near the park entrance was a meadow, or what I thought was a meadow because I'm from the Valley, and we don't have those.

The next part of this story played out like a movie. A disembodied voice said, "Look!" And everyone knew to look that way. There, running through the meadow with his backpack bouncing, a pink flag tied to it, was Derek. He made his way to the bus. By this point, Jennifer had gotten off the bus. The two had said about fifteen words to each other this whole trip, and we didn't know what would happen, if she would slap him or strangle him. But no, he ran into her arms and they hugged, because the prodigal son had returned. Everybody on the bus cheered like they do in eighties movies. I swear I even heard an electric guitar playing the *Top Gun* theme. Derek got on the bus, and that's where I learned: never say never.

In Service

AYON WEN-WALDRON

Being the child of immigrants, I've been in service ever since I can remember. I have very few memories of my life in Taiwan, where I was born. My earliest memories are bits and pieces of the trek my parents made to various countries in South America, when I was three, until we settled in Recife, the largest metro city in northeast Brazil.

As any immigrant child will tell you, our parents count on us to help them navigate a new culture and a new system. My parents moved to Brazil without speaking any Portuguese, and their English was poor. I recall seeing them go from a Chinese-to-English dictionary and then from English-to-Portuguese to figure out meanings. They worked hard and went from selling clothes door-to-door to opening a couple of optical-jewelry shops, eventually shifting their business to restaurants.

A vivid service memory I have is of helping my parents kill live chickens on the weekends. They usually brought home two from the market. The chickens were always the colorful ones, called capoeira, very lean, with glistening bluish and gold feathers. While my dad prepped the boiling water, my mom held back the chicken's wings and neck in one hand. With the other hand, she plucked the neck feathers and, in one swift action, cut the featherless area, dropped the very sharp knife, and grabbed the chicken's twitching legs to hold its body upside-down over a bowl filled partway with water to collect its blood. The blood coagulated into a solid form that could be cooked, sliced, and used as an ingredient in dishes. The kids' job was to collect the bloodless dead chickens—after they flopped all over our backyard for several minutes—and dip them into a big metal bucket of boiling water. We held them there long enough to allow us to easily pull the feathers off the entire chicken. The stench was awful, leaving our hands smelly for hours, no matter how much we washed them. My dad took care of the rest, saving whatever organs he could for our meals.

The restaurant businesses flourished and were so successful that my parents expanded into the hospitality business. More specifically, the hotel business, but the type paid by the hour. By-the-hour hotels make up a significant pillar of the hospitality industry in Brazil and are definitely not taboo. You see, there—and, I daresay, in the rest of the world—unless you belong to the higher echelon, adults usually don't move out of their parents' home until they get married. And you can't disrespect your parents, your family, by bringing anyone into the home to have sex. Especially in urban areas, we lived in small quarters with thin walls.

Privacy is extremely important to the clientele at these hotels. While cheating is not openly accepted and divorce, as well as violence, occurs as a result of it, everyone knows it happens all the time. I think it has to do with the ratio of women to men: something like four women to one man. Okay, I'm exaggerating, but it's high compared to most countries. I shouldn't stereotype, but as my Brazilian girlfriends married to Americans say, Brazilian men are great for bed but not for life. These hotels are surrounded by high walls topped with charred broken glass to keep people out. When a couple drives up to the entrance, they're faced with a long, sliding gate and a security station. Every unit comes with a garage and a gate that lifts to let the car in and closes as soon as it's parked. Each garage has a dedicated set of stairs leading to the bedroom unit above it, so that couples don't have to face any of the guests or employees. To give you a sense of the privacy required, when I delivered room service meals, I opened a small window, put the order through, closed the window, and pushed a button to let the couple know the order was ready. They opened the window from their bedroom and retrieved the meal.

My parents' hotels were popular because they served Chinese menu options. Brazilians love Chinese food; it's considered gourmet over there, especially in the northeast region of the country. I was the kitchen helper, too. Since the key to Chinese cooking is in the prep, I did lots of chopping, dicing, and slicing so that the ingredients were ready for the quick cooking in a hot wok. My dad bragged that our Chinese food was so good that we fulfilled the most carnal, basic human pleasures: to eat amazing food and have sex. Both can lead to orgasmic experiences and unforgettable memories.

The bedrooms were built to maximize the couple's pleasure for the hour—or however long they chose to pay—with mirrored ceilings, vibrating beds, Jacuzzis, couple's showers with all sorts of jets, lots of porn DVDs, oils and gels, toys. You get the picture. Depending on your perspective, it could be "oh, so awesome" or "oh, so cheesy." But my parents were super proud of the business. So much so that when I took my husband to visit them in Recife—before we had kids—my parents couldn't understand why we didn't want to lodge in one of their rooms. "Stay...we want grandchildren soon!"

When we returned to Recife from our U.S. college summer breaks, our father had us bring the latest DVD sets of porn movies. They were so precious that we had to pack them with our carry-on bags. We dreaded whenever security would inspect our luggage. Once the DVDs were discovered, the security guy or gal would look up with this amazed and amused smirk. I'm sure they wondered why these angel-faced youngsters were carrying such kinky cargo. So embarrassing. We just shrugged our shoulders and, if asked, said it was a special order for relatives. It was too embarrassing to say it was business-related.

I'm glad my parents put me to work at a young age and that we had such interesting summer jobs. My parents started from almost nothing and worked their way up to become financially secure, enabling them to give each of their kids an American education debt-free. They worked hard to give us a better life than they had, to be decent people who contribute our services to the well-being of our family, our community, and our society. And for that, I'm deeply grateful.

Reckoning with Racism

BRIA WOODS

As a child, I remember hearing my peers say that I wasn't really Black or that I was an oreo. I've been called an oreo my entire life. I'm in my midtwenties now, and people still call me that. Some of the reasons I've been called an oreo—which means Black on the outside, white on the inside—are that I'm well spoken or so educated. Or because I'm a vegetarian. Because I listen to the Jonas Brothers. Someone even went so far as to say I'm not really Black because I know who my father is.

What's interesting is that I've heard this from both my white and my Black peers. I wasn't Black enough for either group, but I'm clearly not white, so where did that leave me? A lot of my peers, and even teachers and people I looked up to, perpetuated this idea that "don't worry, you're not *really* Black." They said it as if they were congratulating me. Oh, congratulations, you've evaded some kind of second-rate existence. When I moved to San Antonio in 2006, I went to a predominantly white middle school in northeastern San Antonio, and that was when I started to wonder, was my Blackness a problem? One of the girls in my seventh-grade English class used to ask me all these strange questions: "Do you shower? What do you eat? Do you have a mother and a father? Why does your hair look like that?" It was the first time I felt othered.

Unfortunately, I didn't have the vocabulary we have now. We didn't have a lot of these words in 2006, even the word "microaggression." A lot of the concepts and vocabulary surrounding race relations have entered our lexicon in the past five or so years. This is relatively new.

The only currency children have is social acceptance. I didn't want to rock the boat or seem uncool, so I just laughed, like, ha-ha, yeah, I'm not really Black. What I didn't understand is that it was impacting not only my racial identity but also my relationships and friendships. For so long, I was afraid to even associate with other Black kids. I thought, *Oh no, are my teachers going to think that I'm stereotypically Black? Are they going to think I'm bad? Are they going to think less of me if I'm hanging out with the Black kids that fit the stereotype they say I don't exhibit?* It wasn't until I moved to another country that I had my first Black best friend. I had Black friends growing up, of course, but there was always an unspoken distance between us. I think many Black children thought I looked like a duck but didn't quack like one. Again, I wasn't Black enough in their eyes. I moved to London after I graduated from Trinity University, and it was the first time I could just be me. I didn't have to be Black first, or even a woman first. I could walk into a room and be Bria. That's when I started to understand that, wait a minute, I think I've been lied to. Blackness isn't just this small stereotype; it's more than that. It was in the years I lived abroad that I was able to see how racism and prejudice in the United States look from the outside, through the eyes of my diverse group of friends overseas. The truth of the matter is: the world is watching.

Once I returned to the United States, I had a much better view of my personal identity. I have many Black friends I'm very close with now. I understand that Blackness is varied—and not only for myself. No two Black people are the same. We are individuals. I've recognized this for myself, but it's also something I want to impart to anybody reading. Number one, Black people are more than stereotypes. And number two, understand that our words matter. What you say matters, especially if you're talking to young or impressionable individuals. Be mindful of what you're saying even if you think it's in jest. Let's perpetuate positive and becoming narratives about Black people.

At the end of the day, yes, I am Black. I am a woman. I am American. I am all these things, but truly, I'm just Bria.

Contributors

Heather Armstrong is a former TV news reporter who works for the government. She lives in El Salvador.

Tanveer Arora is an IT professional and comedian. He has been nominated Best Comedian in Texas twice in row and starred in the award-winning short film *En Route*.

Jennie Badger is a native of Cuero, Texas, and has lived in San Antonio since graduating from Trinity University. She has worked in public relations, practiced law, and directed children's musicals.

Kiran Kaur Bains is president and chief executive officer of SA2020, a nonprofit that drives progress toward a shared community vision in San Antonio. She previously worked in international development and peacebuilding in South Asia and East Africa.

Marion Barth was born in Chicago. She has volunteered as a leader for the Boy Scouts and the Girl Scouts and for the Air Force Family Service, the American Red Cross, and her church.

Sheila Black is the author of five poetry collections, most recently *Radium Dream*, and the coeditor of *Beauty Is a Verb: The New Poetry of Disability*. She lives in San Antonio.

Barbara Collins Bowie, a civil rights activist and poet, is founder and executive director of the Dr. Bowie, BC Bowie Scholarship Foundation, which implements Black History Month and performing arts after-school programs.

Norma Elia Cantú is the Norine R. and T. Frank Murchison Distinguished Professor of the Humanities at Trinity University. Her most recent book is *Meditación Fronteriza: Poems of Love, Life, and Labor.*

Kelly Grey Carlisle is an associate professor of English at Trinity University and the author of the memoir *We Are All Shipwrecks.* She lives in San Antonio.

Cary Clack is a columnist and editorial board member at the *San Antonio Express-News*. His work has appeared in the *New York Times*, *Texas Monthly*, and the *Texas Observer* and in *The Year's Best Sports Writing 2021.*

Jess Elizarraras is a Rio Grande Valley native and the executive producer for MySA.com. She has also worked at the *San Antonio Express-News* and the *San Antonio Current.*

Georgia Erck is a San Antonio writer. She is winner of the San Antonio Book Festival's Pitchapalooza and has shared personal stories at *Listen to Your Mother* and *Stories Run Amok.*

Tiffany Farias-Sokoloski is an associate professor of instruction at the University of Texas at San Antonio and founder of San Antonio Girls Rock Camp, a nonprofit that seeks to empower girls through music.

Elizabeth Fauerso is a longtime San Antonio resident and the chief executive officer of Potluck Hospitality, responsible for conceiving and operating food, beverage, and entertainment concepts at the Pearl and beyond.

Everett L. Fly is a San Antonio native and licensed landscape architect. His honors include the 2014 National Humanities Medal and the 2021 Daughters of the American Revolution Historic Preservation Medal.

Larry Garza is a comedian and founding member of the sketch group Comedia A Go-Go. He is a winner of the Funniest in South Texas contest and a finalist in the Funniest in Texas and World Series of Comedy contests.

Lorenzo Gomez III is a community builder, author, and public speaker. A former director at Rackspace Technology, he is the cofounder of WeTree, a mental health engagement application.

Mike Knoop is a prospect researcher in advancement services at Trinity University and holds a degree in library science. He has lived in San Antonio for more than twenty years.

David W. Lesch is the Ewing Halsell Distinguished Chair of History at Trinity University and the author or editor of sixteen books, most recently *A History of the Middle East Since the Rise of Islam*.

Rey Lopez is a native San Antonian and a graduate of Trinity University. He works for a financial services company that assists the families of those who have experienced the loss of a loved one.

Vanessa Martinez is a San Antonio native and community activist. She lives on the city's South Side.

Collin McGrath studied English and creative writing at Trinity University and received dual master's and master of fine arts degrees in children's literature from Simmons College.

Joaquin Muerte is a founding member of the San Antonio bands Los Nahuatlatos, Eddie and the Valiants, and the SanAntunes. He is a traditional *danzante conchero* and a community outreach specialist with Health Confianza.

Sanford Nowlin is the editor-in-chief of the *San Antonio Current* and a touring musician. He is the author, as

Sanford Allen, of the historical horror novel *Deadly Passage* and numerous works of short fiction.

Wendy Sheldon Rigby is a San Antonio native and graduated from Trinity University with degrees in broadcast and print journalism.

Rubio was born and raised on San Antonio's West Side and serves as a mentor with the San Antonio Street Art Initiative. His artwork has been exhibited at the San Antonio Museum of Art, the McNay Art Museum, and Contemporary at Blue Star.

Jonathan Ryan is an Irish-Texan attorney who led the immigrant rights organization RAICES from 2008 to 2021. He lives in San Antonio.

Yara Samman is in medical school at the University of Texas Medical Branch, where she cofounded a project for refugee health care and was awarded a Schweitzer Fellowship.

John Phillip Santos is an author, journalist, public artist, and documentary media producer. He teaches mestizo cultural studies at the University of Texas at San Antonio.

Whitley Strieber was born and raised in San Antonio. He is the author of numerous books, including *Communion*, *A New World*, and, most recently, *Jesus: A New Vision*.

Barbara S. Taylor is a professor of infectious diseases and the associate dean of the University of Texas Health Science Center at San Antonio's MD/MPH program. Her work focuses on increasing access to care in South Texas and Latin America.

Michael Taylor writes the weekly "Smart Money" column for the *San Antonio Express-News* and *Houston Chronicle* and is the author of *The Financial Rules for New College Graduates*.

Kirsten Thompson is a Texas native with family roots extending to Haiti and Louisiana.

Clay Utley, a San Antonio native, is a pastor at Tapestry Church and a website sales development representative.

Cristina Van Dusen was born in Mexico City. She is a certified nurse midwife and works at Planned Parenthood in San Antonio.

Eddie Vega is a poet, spoken-word artist, storyteller, educator, and author of *Chicharra Chorus*. He is the recipient of a 2021 Luminaria Artist Foundation literary arts grant and winner of the Southern Fried Poetry Slam's 2022 Haiku Death Match.

Ayon Wen-Waldron teaches at Trinity University, where she graduated with a bachelor's degree in finance. She worked for twenty-five years managing marketing for major brands.

Bria Woods is a photojournalist, radio host, and artist based in San Antonio. She holds a bachelor's degree in communication from Trinity University and a master's in multimedia broadcast journalism from the University of Westminster in London.

Acknowledgments

This book would not have been possible without the incredible community we have in San Antonio. We want to thank all the storytellers who came forward—sometimes at the spur of the moment—as well as the audience members who come to *Worth Repeating* events month after month to hear these stories. We also want to thank the 80/20 Foundation for their partnership from the beginning.

Absolutely vital to *Worth Repeating* are the members of our amazing Storyboard, past and present, who look for tall tales and true anecdotes, coach storytellers, help host, take tickets, pour refreshments, and cheer along the way. Special thanks to the staff at Texas Public Radio, especially Paul Flahive for having the inspiration, Joyce Slocum for originally believing in the program, and Tori Pool, Robert Salluce, Rob Martinez, Ben Henry, and the marketing and events team who work to keep the show alive.

Extra thanks to Elizabeth Motes for helping transcribe and edit initial drafts, and to our family and friends. This book is dedicated to all the stories in San Antonio still waiting to be heard. We're coming for you. Submit your story at tpr.org/wr.

Paul Flahive is Texas Public Radio's first accountability reporter and has worked in public radio and media from Texas to Alaska. His work has been heard on *All Things Considered, Morning Edition, Marketplace, Science Friday*, and *Here and Now* and has been included in winning entries for two Edward R. Murrow Awards. Flahive founded *Worth Repeating* in 2015 and produced it until 2020.

Tori Pool is a Texas writer and comedian and the events manager at Texas Public Radio, where she produces *Worth Repeating* and other community events. She is a two-time nominee for the *San Antonio Current*'s Best Stand-Up Comic and coauthor of the card game *Latino Card Revoked*. A regular at Texas comedy clubs, she has opened for Cristela Alonzo, Mo Amer, Drew Carey, and Tom Green.

Burgin Streetman is a writer and the assistant director of Trinity University Press. She previously worked as publishing coordinator for the Jim Henson Company and director of marketing and publicity for Artisan Books. Her writing has appeared in the *San Antonio Express-News*, *San Antonio Current*, and *San Antonio Report*. She is on the Storyboard of *Worth Repeating* and lives in San Antonio.